The
Twilight of Treaties

MAPS

I

THE TWILIGHT OF TREATIES

In different parts of the world, so dissimilar as the Polar regions, South America, and the Far East, during the past few years diplomatic difficulties have arisen which are oddly alike in their origin.

Over a certain territory, a State possesses either time-honoured historical rights or recent treaty rights: in any case, title-deeds of possession which nobody has ever disputed. This territory, however, is remote or uninhabited, and its owner has not administered it or, sometimes, even occupied it. Subjects of a neighbouring State settle in it, exploit its timber, organise fishing or hunting bases, and even construct railways. Then, one day, they hoist their national flag over the colony which they have founded, and either 'annex' the territory to their own country or proclaim its independence. Their Government, after more or less hesitation, endorses their action. So a new 'question' is raised, which may easily degenerate into a *casus belli*.

A republic given to chronic revolution or, again, an all but abandoned annex of a crumbling empire, with which its link has ceased to be more than nominal, becomes a danger to a whole region of the globe. Some strong Power intervenes, restores order, reorganises the public finances, constructs railways, and

develops the country.   Under its aegis, one State
proceeds to disappear, and another State is born.

There is nothing unprecedented in all this.   Nor is
there even anything quite peculiar to our own time in
the further fact that, more often than not, the new
occupants do not dispute the rights of the old owners.
But what does seem characteristic of our own period is
that the new-comers regard their proceeding as
perfectly legitimate if it is of practical advantage to
themselves or to the territories which they have
politically remodelled.   In the same way, the despoiled
State, though it asserts that its rights are unquestionable, often shows itself ready to discuss them and come
to a compromise with its adversary, not so much
because it bows to force as because it does not itself
seem any too sure about its right to a possession which
another party appears to be better fitted to turn to
account.

Here is something new, and it has a bearing much
wider than that of the cases in point.   For what it tends
towards is the annulment of rights of ownership, even
admitted rights, if the property is not developed; or,
as we may soon say, if possession is not justified by
development.

Again, we have seen non-territorial treaties concluded
for a term of years, and then, long before their expira-
tion, one of the parties to them declaring that they
were incompatible with changes in the economic and
political sphere which had meanwhile taken place –
and here, too, the aggrieved party has shown itself
ready to compromise.

For that matter, ever since the treaties of 1919 and
1920 were signed, what has been in progress ? There

has not even been any attempt to put certain parts of them into force. Their financial clauses have been periodically 'adapted' to the economic situation, real or supposed, of the parties concerned. What, in short, have those bound by these treaties been doing but gradually getting out of them, just like conjurors out of any number of sealed bonds, and suddenly presenting themselves free before the eyes of an astonished audience ?

All this reveals a profound change in accepted ideas about the meaning, and the value, of titles of sovereignty, whether they be historical or based on recent treaties. Nevertheless, odd as it may seem, we cannot accuse our contemporaries of being any more contemptuous than their forefathers of treaties which they have inherited, or of the undertakings which they themselves have given. Apart from moral principles – and there is no proof that such principles used to exist and have now disappeared – the conviction is universal that contracts are no less essential between nations than they are between individuals, and that there is no security for anybody if everybody does not respect his own signature. It may be added, to the credit of the men who hoped to inaugurate a reign of peace after the war, that the supremacy of force was for nearly fifteen years more generally disowned – at least in words – than it had ever been before. Most of those who, about 1934, once more ventured to vaunt the virtues of militarism, still felt bound to justify themselves, in the eyes of world opinion, by claiming that their armament was essential for the defence of some 'sacred right,' whose recognition it was impossible to secure otherwise than by resort to arms.

In fact, the tendency of our time – a tendency more and more marked – is to regard treaties, contracts, agreements, titles of sovereignty of every kind, as documents that must, from time to time, be brought into harmony with the evolving material with which they are concerned.

For that matter, it is undeniable that contracts may, in the long run, become simply incapable of execution in their original form. There are even such things as contracts signed by parties who have ceased to exist. In strict law, these contracts nevertheless remain valid, and some legal practitioners refuse to do more than annotate or interpret their terms.

That is precisely what is making our contemporaries lose their respect for contracts. They come to look upon them as no more than dead things, blocking the path of evolution, which have to be circumvented in order to get on: parchments which any swollen-headed militarist would have a fine time turning into scraps of paper.

For this reason, it seems utterly anachronistic to regard jurists as modern judges in Israel, arbiters of the peace of the world, instead of what they really are: namely, technicians – technicians, to be sure, almost always of high professional competence and perfect honesty, but nevertheless no more than expert consultants, just in the same way as are economists, financiers, generals, geographers, or engineers.

International relations cannot be regulated solely from the juridical point of view; for, if texts drafted by jurists are as immutable, as intangible, as tablets dictated on some Sinai, a day is almost inevitable when harmony between their spirit and reality will be broken, and then you must mobilise to enforce respect

The
Twilight of Treaties

BY

Y. M. GOBLET

TRANSLATED FROM THE FRENCH OF
' LE CRÉPUSCULE DES TRAITÉS '

BY

WARRE BRADLEY WELLS

KENNIKAT PRESS
Port Washington, N. Y./London

THE TWILIGHT OF TREATIES

First published in 1936
Reissued in 1970 by Kennikat Press
Library of Congress Catalog Card No: 70-110930
SBN 8046-0913-6

Manufactured by Taylor Publishing Company   Dallas, Texas

CONTENTS

for the letter of them. Or else, when that day comes, the League of Nations will be constrained to renounce execution of its jurisconsults' decisions: not so much for lack of police as because its decrees are not based upon a critical study of realities, of present-day facts.

Take, for example, the war which, from 1931 to 1935, caused such bloodshed to South America. It was natural and proper that, as a basis of discussion with Paraguay, Bolivia should take either the old colonial frontier of the royal *Audiencia* of Charcas, or the treaties which she signed with the River Plate Republic, but which the Parliament at Asuncion never ratified. But no League of Nations, no Hague Tribunal, no American Conference, no arbiter could secure, merely by its moral authority, respect for any judgment maintaining the frontier of the sixteenth-century *audiencia* as the modern frontier, simply on the ground – however valid it may be juridically – that the Bolivian Republic is the heir of that *audiencia*. Only the Bolivian army could execute that judgment; and it would have to do so by force.

On the other hand, if the League of Nations makes a full investigation of the territory in dispute; if it takes into account the intrinsic economic value of this territory, its extrinsic value to the Republic which it links with the River Plate and the Atlantic, and finally the capacity of each of the parties concerned to develop this territory, then the League of Nations is in a position to say whether the letters patent of the sometime Spanish sovereigns should be maintained, or modified, or annulled in the twentieth century. Both international opinion and national opinion will respect its judgment;

and either party, if it treats such a judgment as null and void, will do itself a moral disservice which no advantage gained by military action can offset. For this judgment will be based upon tangible facts; and they alone sanctify the letter of treaties in the eyes of men of to-day. Better still, in such a case, the League of Nations will present itself as something it is conscious it ought to be, but has not yet become: an assembly of representatives of the nations entrusted with seeing that the evolution of international life be not falsified either by fraud or by force.

Never has such a conception of international relations been more essential than it is at this moment, when all contracts are being called in question, and 'revision of treaties' – meaning the treaties which remade the map of Europe and touched up the map of the rest of the world at many points – may become a task for the near future. Whether these treaties be good or bad, whether you defend them or attack them, in either case you must put yourself in a position to give chapter and verse for your argument, not merely in the juridical sphere of discussion of texts, but also in the realistic sphere of the facts which these texts try to regulate.

If debate be confined to texts and their annotation; if each side, backed by its legists, sticks more and more stubbornly to formulae, then no understanding, no arbitration will be possible, and war will inevitably come. If, on the other hand, judgment be based on knowledge of the natural elements in the case, geographical and human, economic and political, then solutions will be fair, and they will be accepted and supported by international opinion.

It may, perhaps, be said that, in the case of recent great international trials – the trial before the Privy Council of the dispute between Newfoundland and Canada about the coast of Labrador; the trial before The Hague Tribunal of the dispute between Denmark and Norway about East Greenland; and the trial before the League of Nations of the dispute between China and Japan about Manchuria – the advocates of the respective sides took their stand on geographical documentation. This is true; but this documentation was drawn up by the interested parties, and it was examined by judges who had no training in the criticism of documents dealing with political geography.

In the case of Manchuria, the Lytton report was disinterested and objective, but it must be added that though this report assembled data for analytical study, the analytical study was not made. The work of the commission of inquiry certainly helped to enlighten international opinion; but, if the League of Nations had had at its disposal the politico-geographical analysis which it might have drawn from the Lytton report and the Japanese and Chinese memoranda, among other sources, it would probably have been moved to act with more prudence; and who knows whether Japan might not still be a member of the League of Nations ?

Recent international affairs convey the impression that over the world is spreading the shadow, if not of a twilight of law, at least of a twilight of treaties. But, if we examine the facts more closely, we shall see that what is really happening is the ending of a certain conception of the relations between nations; a conception almost purely juridical. Proof has now been

and it demonstrates the emptiness of mystical nationalism, which is only too easy to exploit. Geography possesses a natural strength due to continuous contact with
the earth. It helps to keep international life in the
sphere of concrete realities; and it is in this sphere that
the prospects of practical, pacific understanding among
nations are most numerous.

II

POLITICAL GEOGRAPHY
AND SPAGYRIC 'GEOPOLITIK'

IF I were asked to name an unknown science or, what is worse, a misunderstood one, the word 'geography' would at once occur to me. It is misunderstood – and sometimes even denied any existence. Outside specialist circles, you still hear people say: 'A *science* of geography? No; a geographical method, perhaps.'

Very well: for the moment let us content ourselves with a 'method.' Geographers would be quite capable of defending themselves on their own account, if the need arose. But they are already defended by their works, which are at once the most scientific and the most interesting in the world: perhaps, indeed, out of all scientific writing, the kind which appeals most to the non-specialist, but educated, public. The only trouble is that it is fashionable to deplore the 'dry' sequence of names, 'which was all geography meant when I was a boy.' Those who say so overlook how they 'date' themselves.

Ignorance of geography begins with the worthy who mistook Piræus for a person; and not a few contemporary audiences would see nothing funny in it if a Minister of State on the comic-opera stage exclaimed, like the Duke of Newcastle: 'What? Do you mean to say

Cape Breton is an island ? I must go and tell the
King so at once !'

In international politics, and even in domestic affairs,
such ignorance may lead far. France had occasion to
congratulate herself upon it when Chandernagore
remained French because the Foreign Office thought
it was 'an island in America.' But the treaties of 1919
gained nothing by the fact that certain statesmen confused Silesia with Cilicia. Not so long ago, again, a
Polish ambassador was astounded to hear a Minister
of a friendly country grudgingly grant the Polish
Republic a population of seven million.

It may be said that these are mere slips. But no
excuse is admissible for members of Governments and
diplomats who are ignorant about the way in which the
political map is superimposed upon the physical map,
the economic map, and the anthropo-geographical
map. This is exactly like a tailor being ignorant about
the figure and the measurements of a customer for
whom he has to make a suit. There can be no policy
without political geography, and there can be no
political geography without full knowledge of physical geography and human geography.

Unfortunately, if politicians serenely ignore geography, few geographers concern themselves with
political geography. In the programme of the big
geographical congresses, one searches in vain for any
section devoted to political geography. Just as historical geography, the essential foundation of political
geography, is absent from our curricula, so political
geography is but an unimportant appendix to human
geography. This is not through mere forgetfulness.
At the Paris Congress in 1931, I drew the attention of

an eminent foreign colleague to this gap. He replied, in great excitement: 'Don't start that hare ! God knows where it might lead us !'

Now just where was my friend afraid of being led astray ? Political geography has not a good reputation. As Vidal de la Blache – to whom one must always refer when one studies geographical thought – has pointed out, since political geography was the department of geographical science which was most urgently needed, it developed ahead of the other branches of geography, although it derives from them. Nothing could be more contrary to scientific procedure. The result was that this natural science came to be based upon a kind of philosophy. So there grew up a kind of geographical alchemy; and this, instead of giving place to a scientific political geography, engendered geographical 'spagyrics'[1] which have been developed and exploited for political ends.

As early as 1672, Dr. (later Sir) William Petty conceived the idea of basing policy on geographical study of the country concerned. His *Political Anatomy of Ireland* is, in itself, a remarkably complete essay in human geography. Petty clearly planned to base political and economic science, of which he was to be one of the precursors, upon geographical observation. But the extensive documentation which such a method demanded was not undertaken, and perhaps could not be undertaken, at that time. Besides, Petty was too much a man of action to devote his life to cutting stones for a future edifice. Only a few demographic researches were methodically carried out by his friend,

[1] Spagyric medicine was an attempt to found therapeutics on alchemy, magic, and astrology and to discover a universal panacea.

John Graunt. As for Petty, he surrendered himself to speculations in political arithmetic – for which we should have preserved the name 'arithmancy' – and for three centuries they were to turn economic science out of its normal course of development as a natural science.

The eighteenth century, with its 'men of reason and *a priori* systems,' in political geography as elsewhere, elaborated philosophies which were supposed to be valid for all countries and for all mankind. One might just as well imagine a *homo geographicus* or a *homo politicus* as a *homo œconomicus*. Superficial descriptions alternated with nomenclature and statistics – and we know how sceptical Levasseur was about demographic statistics.

Romanticism, by discovering the picturesque side of the earth and of mankind, directed attention to the fruitful idea of geographical environment, which had been confusedly expressed for centuries. But it also launched the idea of race, which was to endow the concept of the nation with a kind of mysticism. Moreover, the idea of the influence of environment, incorrectly observed and exaggerated by literature, led to the triumph of the fantastic theories of geographical determinism. We may discern the first origin of these theories many centuries earlier, at the time of the Renaissance, if not in the Middle Ages; for, if mankind lives under the influence of the stars, why not under the influence of the earth ?

For three centuries geographical science has been in process of formation, passing through mathematical geography to exploration and finally physical geography and human geography as we understand them to-day. But all this geographical science was only to be used as a pretext by modern spagyric geography, which has taken as a basis pseudo-scientific geographical determinism and false ideas of race, and has afterwards crowned the edifice with ideas of Nation and State considered as a metaphysical entity.

The State appears in its modern form in the frontispiece of Hobbes's *Leviathan*. Evolving from the absolute monarchy of the beginning of the eighteenth century to the militarised State of the nineteenth century and the socialised State of the twentieth century, in all its incarnations it remains the same superhuman entity. It is lord of the land, lord of the people; for the people are merely an annex of the land from which they are born. Around the State – or the sovereign in which it is incarnate – crystallise the elements of nationalism. As for the nation, Ernest Lavisse has summed it up with deadly truth: 'Centred on itself, contemplating itself, loving itself, and, when born proud, admiring itself: such is the psychological condition of the modern nation.' This nation, moreover, has its own territory; and the State decides what is its 'indispensable domain' and which countries suit the 'chosen people.'

From nationalism, a fresh hypertrophy of the national entity leads to imperialism. At this stage, some learned pedant is always to be found to demonstrate that the territorial appetites of the State are absolutely justified, and that from the natural order of things, if not perhaps from God Himself, they derive a sacred character. Frederick the Great, for example, could always find some pedant of a jurisconsult to legalise his encroachments and his conquests.

Just such pedants, at the service of the modern State, are to be found in 'spagyrical' geographers – and their 'science' is contemporary *'Geopolitik.'* It is a great pity that this pseudo-science, enlisted in the service of politics, should have come to birth in Germany. It is painful to find it in the country of Ritter and Ratzel, but for whose work true geographical science would not be what it is to-day. For true political geography dates from the *Politische Geographie* which Ratzel based upon scientific observation; and, if everything in Ratzel is not worth preserving, at least this founder of modern political geography formulated some provisional laws and laid down certain principles of procedure.

But nothing differs more from the science founded by Ratzel – who, without realising it, took up Petty's line of thought – than the *'Geopolitik'* which has developed in Germany since the war. Its inventors, for that matter, regard Ratzel as a forerunner whom they have out-distanced by a long way; and they level against him the reproach – rather extraordinary coming from geographers – that he assigned too much importance to geographical factors in the formation of the State. Research in regional geography does not suffice for them; for they must appeal to every kind of science – though, indeed, it is somewhat superfluous thus to justify a conclusion reached in advance. In fact, all they do is to go back, long before Ratzel, to the procedure which discredited political geography at its cradle.

For what they are concerned about is not doing scientific work, but justifying the omnipotence of the State: a State which is represented as a living, conscious entity, with a will of its own and even passions of its own; a State which is more than the sum of the citizens who compose it; a State which exists on its own account, which alone is real, and which is of such a kind that its citizens exist only in it and for it. Here we are back at Saint Anselm's 'universals.' 'Realists' are the same in the twentieth century as in the eleventh century; and the application, if not the origin, of their doctrine is the same. A regular system of State anthropomorphism has been developed, and its cause is served with grim fanaticism.

The 'real' State leads its predestined people. It assimilates minorities which have the bad luck to be born on its sacred territory. Outside this territory it annexes any other territory which is necessary for the expansion of the chosen people. All this shows why a geographical basis is essential; how geography can be twisted to the service of the State; and how *'Geopolitik'* came to be one of the first foundations on which Hitlerian National-Socialism was built.

In fact – even though Scandinavians, for example, are to be found among 'geopoliticians' – *'Geopolitik,'* which at the outset produced works on human geography of real interest, has become more and more a Nazi, a pan-German propaganda machine: an instrument for the construction of the Third Reich, and for the destruction of the 'pseudo-national States, consumptive from birth,' doomed by the 'iron law of geographical influence' to absorption in the Germanic Empire.

Thus *'Geopolitik,'* though it may claim to be the 'guide of world policy' (Dix), the 'geographical conscience of the State' (Hennig), has really lost any scientific character, any objectivity, any true geographical interest. It has become nothing more than an agent of one of those nationalist systems of State mysticism which, in the post-war world, are bringing to life again the very spirit that caused the war. The main importance of all this – if we leave aside its dangerous political consequences – is that the choice of the name '*Geopolitik*' for this pseudo-science has discredited the name of political geography in the eyes of the general public.

To-day, when you say 'political geography,' you are usually taken to mean '*Geopolitik*.' The reader will now understand why, at the Paris Congress in 1931, a geographer belonging to a country which has suffered from German imperialism was so much afraid of any talk about political geography.

All the political sciences without exception, from sociology to diplomacy, from history to political economy, have a geographical basis, just as they have a human basis. So much is self-evident. A few great minds saw this long ago.

If we confine ourselves to moderns, Petty laid down the principle that, if you want to study a country, you must have at your disposal the best map of that country which can be procured. Michelet compares any history without a geographical preface to one of those Chinese paintings in which the ground does not figure and the people seem to float in the air. Ernest Lavisse asked Vidal de la Blache to make a *Tableau de la Géographie de la France*, and made it the first volume of his *Histoire de France* – and this *Tableau* is a masterpiece. The sociologist Durckheim and the geologist de Lapparent join hands. The former declares that the best way of learning the history of nations is to know all about the terrestrial environment in which they live. The latter calls territory 'the substratum of social life,' adding that territory is to that life what the brain is to thought; for collective phenomena vary according to its composition, just as thought varies according to the composition of the brain.

Accordingly, every political science has strong geographical foundations. Every department of geography contributes elements which, specially elaborated for the use of the political sciences, constitute political geography.

Mathematical geography and physical geography give us information about the position, the climate, the soil, and the natural divisions of regions and countries. Human geography makes a demographic, economic, and social tabulation and transfers it to special maps, devoted to ethnography, demography, production, and so on. Here in facts and figures, without any 'literary' trimming, are set down the mutual actions and reactions of mankind and the earth. Historical geography, which demonstrates the evolution and transformation of these reactions by successive maps, is of capital importance. It alone can make us acquainted with successive aspects of the political map of States, and show us how they gradually came to assume their present appearance.

For any study in political geography, therefore, the way must be paved by a twofold exploration of the countries concerned and the relations between them : one exploration in the sphere of space, and another exploration in the sphere of time. This determines its method. It must, before all else, avoid abstractions, for they inevitably lead it astray into metaphysics, of which the example of '*Geopolitik*' shows the danger.

As a science of observation, like all geography – and, for that matter, all political sciences – political geography takes a particular case and makes a geographical analysis of it : not only of its present, but also of different periods, carefully chosen, of its past. So we get, in the first place, a series of anatomical plates, accompanied by descriptions.   Next comes a biological study. After that, especially in the midst of contemporary crises, one sometimes has to make a pathological study, which must be carefully kept distinct from the anatomical study of the normally healthy subject.   Perhaps one may even be led to add to it a chapter on teratology.

What, then, is the precise sphere of political geography ?

It analyses and studies the geographical complexes which occur in the formation and evolution of political groupings possessing a geographical component part – in other words, nations and States.   So much being understood, its present work – for the science is still in its infancy – consists in multiplying subjects of dissection, observation, and analysis.   Only in this way can it pave the way for classification and the future elaboration of inductive laws.

But meanwhile its processes of observation will often be of immediate practical utility.   For such observation alone can provide the essential material for establishing a geographical criticism of nations and States : a criticism that will enable statesmen and diplomats to recognise whether international treaties and transactions are in harmony with the natural phenomena which they have to interpret in the political sphere.

We must, however, be very careful not to confuse political geography with what may be called administrative geography and diplomatic geography; for these latter deal only with the lay-out, and the variations, of internal divisions within States and the external frontiers of States. These are arbitrary manifestations of the will of men, and often even of the enemies of the State concerned. Accordingly, such departments of geography study artificial constructions, which are the work of war and which engender war.

Political geography, on the other hand, studies natural phenomena, and thus paves the way towards peace. For what people quarrel about is, as a rule, something badly understood, something vague, something set forth without objectivity. For this reason, all scientific research works towards peace. But what works most directly of all towards peace is the impartial study of human groupings; their geographical domain and its variations; and the way in which the main subjects of diplomacy and its treaties are written on the soil.

III

EXPERIMENTS IN
POLITICAL GEOGRAPHY IN EUROPE

I. THE SAAR TERRITORY UNDER THE
LEAGUE OF NATIONS

HERE we have a complete experiment, since it has come to an end. Let it not be objected that it ended in failure. The essential thing is that an experiment in political geography has been made; that it continued for fifteen years; that it presented a very clear case of economic interdependence; and that it enabled a politico-geographical complex to function without let or hindrance outside the sphere of any State, and bestowed exceptional prosperity on a human group. The fact that this group, for reasons of a sentimental kind, afterwards chose to merge itself in another complex, which is national and imperial, proves nothing derogatory to the value of free politico-economic units, any more than Fascism or Bolshevism proves anything derogatory to the value of political liberty for nations sufficiently advanced to govern themselves. Nor does this fact affect the legacy to us of an experiment unique in political geography.

THE CREATION OF THE SAAR TERRITORY

The creation of the Saar Territory was the consequence of Germany's cession to France, in full ownership, of the coal-mines in the Saar basin, as compensation for the destruction of the collieries in the north of France and the Pas-de-Calais by the invading German armies. Its birth certificate was Article 49 of the Treaty of Versailles, which stipulated that 'Germany renounces in favour of the League of Nations, in the capacity of trustee, the government of the Territory' (of the Saar). In order that the coal-mines might be worked normally, in the requisite atmosphere of tranquillity, the treaty further prescribed that, for a period of fifteen years dating from its coming into force – that is to say, from January 1921 – the district should be placed under the control of the League of Nations, which would delegate its administration to an international commission consisting of five members, with the collaboration of a local Parliament.

As to the territory bordering on the north-east frontier of France to be thus administered, the seven hundred and forty odd square miles of the *Gebiet* were taken out of the 'circles' of Rhenish Prussia and the Bavarian Palatinate, in such a way that, together with the coal-mines which constitute its *raison d'être*, it also included the outer suburbs of the mining and industrial region: the districts inhabited by the workers in the mines and factories. The Territory thus comprised the 'circles' of Saarbrücken, Saarlouis urban, Saarlouis rural, Ottweiler, and Saint Ingbert, together with, on its northern and eastern boundary, several districts out of the 'circles' of Merzig, Saint Wendel, Homburg, and Zweibrücken, but not the town of Zweibrücken. Most of the eastern boundary was traced on the spot. Thus was constituted an administrative unit embracing three hundred and sixty parishes. It was said of it that with the area of a French *arrondissement* it combined the population of two French *départements*; for its demographic density was five times that of France, and its figure of population rose – especially through the immigration of German workmen attracted by plentiful work and high wages – from 630,000 souls in 1919 to 833,000 in 1933.

It is quite possible, though doubtful, that in the minds of its creators, the politico-geographical organism thus brought into being was nothing more than a coal-mining centre provisionally linked with French economy in order to take the place of the mines of the north of France, as it was thought that these mines would not be workable for a very long time, if ever. The Versailles Treaty stipulated that at the end of fifteen years – that is to say, in 1935 – the people of the Saar, both those resident there and those born there who had emigrated to any part of the world, should be called upon to decide by a plebiscite whether they wished that the Territory should remain under the control of the League of Nations, be restored to Germany, or be annexed to France. This stipulation shows that those who made it were thinking in political terms.

THE SAAR REGION

Something more, in fact, was involved than simply an episode in the 'liquidation' of the war. The Saar Territory was not merely an little artificial political organism arbitrarily entrusted to the League of Nations. Study of its brief life of fifteen years would be valueless if we gave way to the tendency, unhappily so common in our time, to imagine States and administrative divisions as though the dotted lines which surround them were something like the sheer coast of an island isolated from the rest of the world. To get an exact idea of what the *Gebiet* really was, we must consider it in relation to the geographical complex of the Saar region as a whole, of which it formed one of the essential parts.

Here we find ourselves on those 'marches' (border-lands) of Gaul and Germany, where the twentieth century still struggles over the heritage of Charle-magne. It is one of those regions in which geo-graphical factors have possessed in all centuries and for all peoples a capital importance, and exerted on the evolution of history an influence which is often overlooked.

The Franco-German frontier of 1814 placed on the French side the southern and western half – less the 'circle' of Merzig – of what in 1920 was to become the Saar Territory. Accordingly the Saar valley as far as Fremersdorf was French. It required Napoleon, the Hundred Days, Waterloo, and the second Treaty of Paris to deprive France of this frontier, the Saar-brücken mines, and the town of Saarlouis, founded in accordance with a plan drafted by Vauban in 1680, when Louis XIV organised the north of Lorraine, where French colonists, whose names still survive in the region, were prepared to create a new French province.

If we study on a historical map the political vicissi-tudes of the Saar region, if not from the days of the Gauls, at least from the year 999, when the Bishop of Metz received the town of Saarbrücken from the Emperor Otto III, we find ourselves all the time in

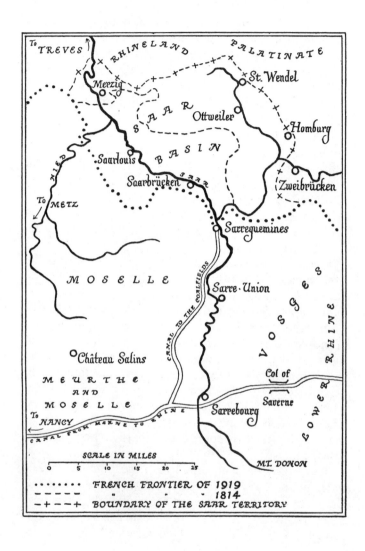

To TREVES   RHINELAND   PALATINATE

Merzig   St. Wendel

S A A R   Ottweiler   Homburg

B A S I N

Saarlouis

To METZ   Saarbrücken   SAAR   Zweibrücken

BLIES

Sarreguemines

M O S E L L E   Sarre · Union

CANAL TO THE COALFIELDS

V O S G E S

L O W E R   R H I N E

Château Salins

M E U R T H E
AND
M O S E L L E   Col of

Saverne

To NANCY   CANAL FROM MARNE TO RHINE   Sarrebourg

MT. DONON

SCALE IN MILES

0   5   10   15   20   25

· · · · · · · ·   FRENCH FRONTIER OF 1919
– – – – –   "   ·   ·   1814
– + – – +   BOUNDARY OF THE SAAR TERRITORY

Lorraine land: an intermediary zone where opposing influences periodically advance and retreat. This situation, indeed, is in the order of nature itself, which presents the physical map as a theme whose variations on the political map, if they are to be lasting, must always conform to its main lines.

This Saar region, in fact, consists of the eastern and northern part of Lorraine, whose rich plains and salt-pits are bounded to the east, for a distance of some sixty miles, by the upper course of the river, which flows at the foot of the Vosges in the district where the roads from Lower Alsace emerge. In the neighbourhood of Sarreguemines, and as far as Merzig, the Saar runs west-north-west for the forty odd miles of the middle part of its course. Here is the most active and the richest part of its valley, the part that cuts through the coal deposit, which is estimated to be nearly five thousand feet thick, with a potential yield of twelve milliards of tons.

This was the centre of the Territory, whose soil was in part an extension of the Lorraine plateau, on both banks of the Saar, into the fertile districts of the Saargau and the Bliesgau, separated by a wooded region. Further north, beyond the Köllerthal, whose meadows have become mines, it rose towards the highest point in the region, the Schaumberg, and the forest-covered hills of the Hochwald and the Birkenfeld.

The Territory thus possessed no physical unity, apart from the depression in the carboniferous area. Similarly it possessed none of those frontiers which people call 'natural.' The river and the escarpment in which the plateau region ends to the north have only partly preserved their military importance in the days

when Vauban, in the course of plotting his Luxem-
bourg-Phalsburg defensive line, set Saarlouis to guard
the crossing of the Saar.

Ever since ancient times, the wide valley of the Saar
has been a meeting-place for the people of the neighbouring forest regions: those of Lorraine, the Westrich
and the Rhenish Palatinate. Saarbrücken is situated
at the point from which the Saar was once navigable,
and for centuries traffic followed the routes which met
there: the river and road route taken by the salt of
Lorraine; the route from Flanders and the maritime
Low Countries to Alsace and Switzerland – in fact, the
route from the Atlantic to the Alps, which was so
prosperous from the Middle Ages to the nineteenth
century that in the neighbourhood of Sarreguemines
it was called the *Goldene Strasse* (the 'golden road'); and
finally the 'German routes,' still very much alive and
now complemented by railways – Saarbrücken is the
centre of a railway network – from Metz to the Rhine
by way of the valleys of the Saar, the Blies, and the
Schwarzbach. Accordingly the Territory, in its status
from 1920 onwards, became a kind of Customs 'lock'
between France and Germany, and then an autonomous centre of international trade.

The economic system and population of the Saar Territory

The economic character of the Saar in modern times
manifested itself at the beginning of the nineteenth
century, when coal became the fuel for iron-founding.
It asserted itself still more about the middle of that
century, when railways multiplied. Then unity between the mineral, industrial, and agricultural regions

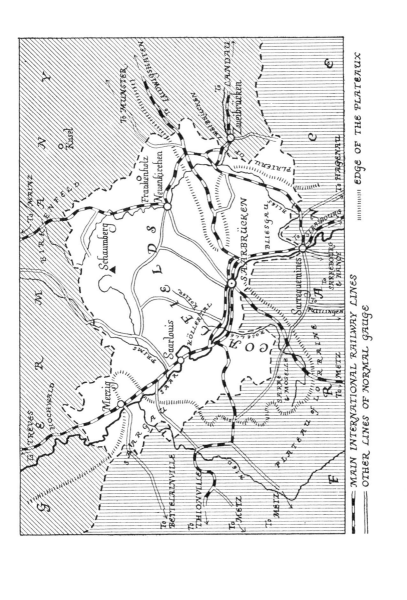

MAIN INTERNATIONAL RAILWAY LINES — — — EDGE OF THE PLATEAUX
OTHER LINES OF NORMAL GAUGE

was created by mining. The productive part of the coalfield starts from near Kusel; but Prussia, perhaps influenced by the Ruhr, never put great energy into the development of the Saar. From Frankenholz, the most northerly pit, however, the coalfield was worked as far as the Prims. Further south the seam becomes lost underground; but it becomes workable again in the Lorraine Basin at the Petite Rosselle, Sarre-et-Moselle, and La Houve mines.

Industrially the collieries meant a second birth for the Saar region. Its coal was exported to eastern France, and utilised on the spot in the coke-works and iron foundries which treated the Lorraine ores. Only a distance of some sixty miles separated the fuel from the 'minette.'[1] Unfortunately the organisation and equipment of the water-route which linked them left much to be desired. Similarly, at the other extreme of the Saar's industrial life, in the case of the overseas export which was indispensable to it because the Ruhr and Lorraine ousted it from neighbouring markets, the same kind of insufficiency made transport to the over-distant ports inconvenient and expensive. But, if the Saar had remained autonomous and continued to enjoy free trade, its future would have been assured by a natural process of evolution towards the production of coke gas, electric current, finished metallurgical products, machinery, and mechanical contrivances, in whose manufacture the Saar workers display a skill which seems innate in them, and is, in fact, due to a long tradition.

Its working population, consisting of miners who remain countrymen and conservatives, and metallurgists who conform more to our idea of the modern

[1] Minette : phosphorus oolitic iron ore of Lorraine.

worker, gives the Saar a very pronounced demographic character. The density of population exceeds 2,500 to the square mile in the mining centre. Around it extends a wide halo consisting of crowded suburbs and countryside still agricultural, which provides a percentage of the workers and a part of the food supply. But the soil is poor. As in the Ruhr, the population map retains the impression of times earlier than the age of coal. What Vauban said remains true: 'The Saar possesses nothing but overgrown villages.' The sole exception to-day is Saarbrücken. On the other hand, the old towns in the rich Rhenish-Westphalian plain have gone on growing.

Since the soil of the Saar can provide its population with barely two months' food supply, Saarbrücken and its region have always had to buy milk, vegetables, fruit, and meat from the Moselle district of Lorraine. In 1934, the Territory purchased only 230 million francs' worth of food from Germany, whereas it purchased 400 million francs' worth from France. At this figure its importation from France, which at one time reached 700 million francs, became stabilised. Customs duties had nothing to do with this: the cause was solely that French prices were more favourable than German.

ECONOMIC INTERDEPENDENCE

Importation of ore and food from Lorraine; exportation of its own coal and metallurgical products – these constitute the basis of the economic interdependence of what used to be the Saar Territory. Here geographical analysis brings us down to bed-rock, and reveals to us its natural markets, in accordance with which it must organise its external relations.

We find that the economic activity of the Saar has always been directed towards the regions to the south of it: Lorraine and Alsace, and, beyond them, eastern France, Switzerland, and Italy. The geographical position of the Saar and Lorraine rendered the coal of the former and the iron ore of the latter complementary to each other. Just as, before the war, the Saar owed its prosperity to its inclusion in the same *Zollverein* as Alsace-Lorraine, so the prosperity of the Territory from 1920 to 1935 was bound up with its customs union with France. For the Saar has experienced unusual good fortune: it has seen the frontiers of the regions with which it has vital links in common transformed in such a way that the political régimes that succeeded one another both bestowed upon it a customs status in perfect harmony with the natural conditions of its economic development, and that neither of them put any obstacle in the way of its trade with its natural suppliers and customers.

This constant economic orientation of the valley of the Saar is a factor in human geography worthy of note. It is a factor all the more remarkable because in this old Lotharingia, where for twelve centuries so many territorial arrangements succeeded one another, politicians very often ignored the natural vocation of the region, cutting it up arbitrarily and changing its allegiance with complete indifference to economic realities. The League of Nations, for its part, gave fifteen years of prosperity to its first Territory.

The Saar region also presents another source of

interest to the student of political geography. It is a characteristic type of the frontier region. Old-time diplomacy and geography used to see in watercourses what they called 'natural frontiers.' Nevertheless, both banks of the middle Saar valley were assigned to France in 1814 and to Prussia in 1815. Did those who drafted the treaty of 1919 conceive the idea of a neutral frontier region, open to both countries at once? From the geographical point of view, the idea is an attractive one, if only from the economic and demographic results of its application.

THE END OF THE EXPERIMENT

The plebiscite of January 13, 1935, put an end to the experiment of the Saar Territory, for nine-tenths of the electors voted in favour of its restoration to Germany. For some time earlier, the result of the voting had not been in doubt, if indeed it ever really was.

In this region, once French in its race, its culture, and its allegiance, a century of Prussianisation has destroyed almost every trace of its origin. The Second Reich showed the utmost solicitude for the people of the Territory, while France took no interest in the way that they might vote in 1935. Later, however, it was believed that the Hitlerian régime would greatly impair the quasi-unanimity with which they were expected to pronounce in favour of Germany.

The report of the Governing Commission to the League of Nations for the third quarter of 1933 described Nazi propaganda as having been most provocative, and as now manifesting itself 'in a ceaseless campaign of threats, denunciations, and camouflaged boycott, directed against inhabitants of the Territory who are suspected of not sharing the ideas of the National-Socialist Party.'   Accordingly, there was said to be an increasing number of Saar people who would like to see a few more years of the *status quo* : long enough for the state of affairs in Germany to change.   Moreover, Herr Hitler's anti-Catholic attitude disquieted Saar adherents of the Church of Rome.   Partisans of the *status quo* even hoped for intervention on the part of the Vatican; but the Vatican, being well informed about the strength of the Nazis, refrained from taking sides, and its silence played its part in the immense Hitlerian majority.   On the other hand, the campaign for the maintenance of the *status quo* was poorly and clumsily organised, and it was compromised by alliance with the Socialists and even the Communists.

So the Nationalists need not have done what they did : import 'natives of the Saar,' at great expense, from all over the Reich, and even from America. Even without them, the plebiscite would have been a great success for Germany and, in short, for Herr Hitler.   Such small opposition as was manifested served only to give this success all the character of a Nazi 'Marne.'   That was an easy victory, too; but, on the morrow of it, the Third Reich did not hesitate long about officially regarding the Treaty of Versailles as a scrap of paper.

Nevertheless, the experiment of the League of Nations in the Saar was not submitted to the test of judgment by the people.   For it was not on this experiment that the plebiscite of January 13, 1935, was held. The voting was on a purely sentimental question, whereas the real problem was administrative and economic in character.   On several occasions, both

the German Chamber of Commerce at Saarbrücken
and the 'Franco-Sarroise' Chamber of Commerce,
without expressing any political opinion, gave it to be
understood that they desired to maintain the relations
developed since 1920 between the Saar and Lorraine –
in other words, France – which were making the Territory's fortune, and constituted, in fact, only an extension of the pre-war relations between the Saar region
and the 'Reichsland.' What else was to be expected ?

As a territory under the League of Nations, the Saar
was a free market for one hundred million souls,
German and French, an economic 'lock' between
two great States. If the Saar became French, it would
lose the munificence and the custom of Germany.
Now that it has become German, it is separated from
the suppliers who fed both its population and its
industry.[1] On the other hand, it cannot recover the
position it held before 1914 in the Reich ; for Germany,
now that she has lost Alsace-Lorraine, is powerless to
restore the Saar to the economic complex of which it
formed a part. At the same time, the Saar finds itself
once more confronted by its eternal, and successful,
competitor, the Ruhr, now augmented by the Aix-la-
Chapelle Basin: the Ruhr which earlier prevented it
from obtaining a canal linking it to the Rhine.

So the practical result of the plebiscite of January 13,
1935, for the Saar will be that it will be compelled to
modify its industries and devote itself, to quote the
Frenchman who has perhaps made the closest study of
it, M. Capot-Rey, to 'the "*ennoblissement*" of coal, the

[1] Despite a customs arrangement – which in any case is only temporary – trade between the Saar and France diminished by three-quarters
in the first six months of 1935, while the number of unemployed in the
Saar rose from 36,000 to 60,000.

production of coke gas on a large scale, and the renovation of its minor industries by a cheap fuel.' Finally, its geographical situation will restore it to the thankless rôle of a frontier 'march' between two national States. Nevertheless, it cannot be said that the experiment of the neutral Territory was made in vain.

II. SLESVIG:

SCANDINAVIA'S SOUTHERN 'MARCH'

Since the spring of 1933 and the foundation of the Hitlerian 'Third Reich,' manifestations have been organised in the south of Denmark by Nazis. Having made 'Geopolitik' one of the bases of their doctrine, they are exerting themselves to revive 'Schleswig-Holsteinism' and give it a modern form.

The case of Slesvig is one of those in which old-time policy and diplomacy, by resolutely ignoring the simplest of geographical and human factors, created one of their most confused imbroglios.

The Scandinavian world terminates south of Jutland in a frontier zone very clearly defined; but, as sovereigns ruled at one and the same time over Danish Slesvig and Germanic Holstein, the two duchies have been the subject of age-long struggle between Denmark and Germany.

From the point of view of human geography, the Scandinavian domain, to whose unity witness is borne by runic inscriptions, extends uninterruptedly from the Eider to the Arctic Ocean over southern and northern Jutland, the Danish and Finnish islands, the great Swedo-Norwegian peninsula, the Norwegian islands, Iceland and Greenland. Since as early as

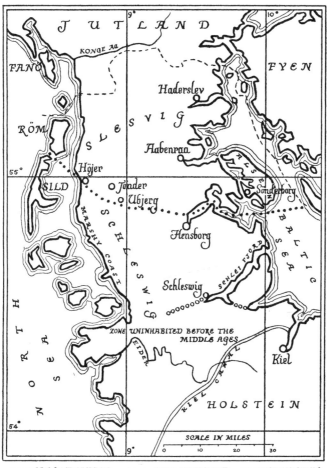

JUTLAND

KONGE AA

FANÖ

RÖM

FYEN

Haderslev

SLESVIG

Aabenraa

55°

Höjer

SILD

Tönder

Sönderborg

Ubjerg

ALSEN

Flensborg

BALTIC SEA

SCHLESWIG

Schleswig

SCHLEI FJORD

ZONE UNINHABITED BEFORE THE
MIDDLE AGES

NORTH SEA

MARSHY COAST

EIDER

Kiel

KIEL CANAL

54°

HOLSTEIN

SCALE IN MILES

| 0 | 10 | 20 | 30 |

9°

- - - - 1864 FRONTIER   • • • • 1920 FRONTIER   ooooo DANEVIRKE prehistoric times the Danes have inhabited not only their archipelago and northern Jutland, but also southern Jutland, which about the thirteenth century came to be called Slesvig, from the name of its capital. Johannes Steenstrup has demonstrated the similarity between Slesvig and Scandinavian place-names, and shown that 'traces of Danish colonisation extend as far as the Eider.'

To the north of this river, as far as Sli (Schlei) Fjord, an uninhabited zone of forest, marsh, heath, and moor formed a natural boundary between the Danish lands and those of the Saxons and the Slavs. Here, in the time of Charlemagne, the Danes constructed the rampart known as the Danevirke. In the deserted zone, which was cleared little by little, Frisians settled to the south-west, and in the thirteenth and fourteenth centuries Germans colonised other parts of it. But the Sli and the Danevirke remained for a thousand years the linguistic frontier, and towards the south the Danish kingdom was defended by the 'march' between the Eider and the Konge Aa, which was well organised and administered by a *jarl* who was usually a relative of the king. The result was that political geography, which was, so to speak, spontaneous, was based on factors of physical geography.

The great vassals of the later Middle Ages and the sovereigns of modern times remodelled States in accordance with political calculations. In 1460 Germanic Holstein was united to southern Jutland, which was purely Danish; and this was acclaimed as a success at Copenhagen. In fact, Slesvig-Holstein, half Danish, half Germanic, corresponded to no reality either geographical or human. It was a creation so artificial that in 1721 Slesvig was politically reunited with Denmark, though it remained administratively linked with Holstein. The Danish kingdom regained its frontier on the Eider; but Germanism retained a sphere of colonisation. The snobbishness of the aristocracy and bureaucratic and ecclesiastical influences made German the language of the country to the south of Flensborg.

In the middle of the nineteenth century, when Prussia and Austria deprived Denmark of Slesvig by force in 1864, the Danish language had for its southern boundary a line running from Flensborg through Tönder to the island of Sild: a line which curved very far southwards in the middle of the peninsula. In the elections in 1867, out of the hundred Slesvig parishes to the north of the Flensborg-Tönder line only one little moorland village, Ravsted, had a German majority – and this was offset by the Danish majority at Karlum, to the south of the line. This coincidence of the linguistic demarcation with the political demarcation conveys the impression that here we are in the presence of a constant anthropo-geographical fact.

When the victory of the Allies in 1918 turned national dreams which four years earlier had seemed unrealisable into a tangible reality, some enthusiasts, most of them foreigners, suggested the creation of a Greater Denmark, with the Sli-Danevirke line as its frontier. The idea was that no Dane should be left outside the national domain. But such had been German colonisation and – during the first few years after 1864 – Danish emigration, that a minority of 250,000 Germans would thus have been incorporated in the kingdom, in which they would have formed 8 per cent of the total population. Denmark wisely refused so dangerous a gift. On October 23, 1918, the Rigsdag expressed the desire that only northern Slesvig, which had remained purely Danish, should be reunited to Denmark. What was the good of Flensborg to Denmark? In 1867 the town had a population of 20,000 souls, and it yielded 1,863 Danish votes and 1,648 German votes. In 1912 it had a population of 70,000 souls, numbered barely 8,000 persons who spoke Danish, and yielded only 456 Danish votes against 11,412 German votes.

This moderation on Denmark's part; her readiness to recognise hard facts, have earned her the compensation that to-day there is no Danish frontier question. The Versailles Treaty line raises no discussion inside the country. For, even with a very exact system of proportional representation, which enables all the German votes to be added together, there is only one German member in the Rigsdag. In northern Slesvig, the plebiscite in 1920 showed 25 per cent of Germans. In the elections in 1932, there was only $13\frac{1}{2}$ per cent of German votes. The reason was that people born in the province but not resident in it – most of them children of German officials who had returned to Germany – were no longer voting; that the number of German officials had greatly diminished; and finally – and this throws a flood of light on the evolution of opinion in Danish Slesvig since the war – that the Germanised Socialists voted not the German Nationalist 'ticket,' but the Danish Socialist 'ticket.'

According to the census of 1930, the population of the territory restored to Denmark totalled 178,000 souls, of whom 150,000 were Danes. Moreover, the so-called German minority is Germanic rather by sentiment than race, for a considerable part of it is made up of Germanised Danes. Thus, in one and the same family, some members of it vote ' Danish ' and other members vote ' German.' The percentage of Germans and pro-Germans is higher in the cities and towns, such as Sönderborg, Aabenraa, Haderslev, and especially Tönder, where it reaches 21.7 per cent, than it is in the country districts, where it averages only 9.7 per cent. Only the village of Höjer (1,083 inhabitants) and the hamlet of Ubjerg (453 inhabitants) have German majorities, and these majorities are quite small (52 per cent and 54 per cent of German votes respectively).

Denmark has treated Slesvig as a regular frontier district, and the different ethnical elements enjoy complete freedom. A number of German officials have even been retained. In the administrative units of Aabenraa, Sönderborg, Tönder, and Haderslev, there are respectively 44, 60, 54, and 31 German-trained schoolmasters, compared with 119, 90, 110, and 131 Danish-trained.

More than ever before, Slesvig is now the southern 'march' of the Scandinavian world. In April 1933, in the course of the commemoration at Dybboel, the windmill outside Sönderborg where the heroes of Denmark fired their last cartridges on April 18, 1864, delegations from Norway, Sweden, Finland, and Iceland were present to testify that here was 'the frontier-guard of Scandinavia.'

On the other hand, it must be pointed out that there is no such thing as a Nazi movement in Slesvig.

There is simply an attempt to resurrect 'Schleswig-Holsteinism,' a manifestation of that antiquated idea which replaces hard facts of physical and human geography by artificial arrangements, calculated to provoke frontier questions and engender war.

Slesvig is one of the places where we can see most clearly how the words 'nationality,' 'nation,' and 'State' designate realities which are different and some-times opposed: three complexes which are not even on the same plane. Prussia and Imperial Germany managed to separate heterogeneous regions from the Danish State, and either to destroy Danish nationality, in a traditionally Scandinavian domain, by a process of Prussification, or to reduce it to the condition of a negligible minority by a process of enforced emigration; for the modern State has means of pressure on men's minds at its disposal which far surpass the ancient State's power to enslave men's bodies.

On the other hand, it is a phenomenon worthy of study and reflection that a national State should be wise enough to renounce the exercise of its historical rights over a part of its traditional domain, just because, in the course of half a century, this province has been denationalised. From this fact, however, we may observe that experimental political geography does not date merely from the establishment of the League of Nations. But in the old days the experiments of the imperialist States were based on force, and had enslavement as their object. What is of interest in connection with the experiments inaugurated in 1919 is that they seek to re-establish the natural order of things, and favour the normal evolution of nations.

Yet, when Sir Walter Layton wrote that Germany

ought to regard the Danish frontier as no less inviolable than the French frontier, the *Schleswische Zeitung*, that organ of Nazi propaganda, made the mocking reply that he 'might wake up one fine day and find that the German-Danish frontier had been changed overnight.' This newspaper omitted to add that *'Geopolitik'* is equipped with resources for justifying such a change 'scientifically' on the morrow.

III. THE AUSTRIAN REPUBLIC AND
THE CONTINENTAL EMPORIUM OF VIENNA

Among all the States which were transformed by the war, Austria is one of those whose economic and political distress has moved even their former enemies. Many people abroad, and even in the country itself, obsessed by sterile regrets for the past and unable to regard the Republic of Austria as anything but an expiatory reincarnation of Austria-Hungary, describe it as 'a hydrocephalous monstrosity, an enormous head on a stunted body.' But it was no inevitable Fate which condemned the new State to be nothing more than a raft made out of rotten planks from the wrecked Habsburg ship *Méduse*, with one-ninth of its population dying of hunger while they awaited rescue by some Nazi pirate.

Austria's misfortunes ever since the Treaty of Saint-Germain have been due to the fact that she has continued to think along the lines of a world peopled by phantoms of the old political complexes, with the German Empire and the Dual Monarchy playing the leading rôles. Once her incarnation in the Austro-Hungarian and some-time Holy Roman Empire was over, she awaited reincarnation in an imperialist

German Republic. So, instead of being a new political entity, the new Austria condemned herself to be no more than a spectre wavering amid phantoms.

Yet this Republic of Austria potentially embodies a new geographical individuality, if not a new type of State, though inadequacy of nomenclature leads it to be confused wrongly with past forms of State. The fact of the matter – and this is what has not been properly realised – is that there is no common measure between the young Republic and the collapsed Empire.

The Dual Monarchy was the perfect type of those Powers which the old-time conquerors and diplomats made up just as they saw fit, by putting fragments of territory and debris of nations together, without taking the trouble to organise a geographically and politically homogeneous State. So it came to be said of Austria-Hungary that she was 'not even a geographical expression.' On the other hand, the Republic of Austria is the most perfect – if the expression is not in danger of seeming ironical – of those national States which looked so fine in our pre-war dreams; for, out of her population of $6\frac{1}{2}$ million, only 160,000 are not German-speaking. To tell the truth, experience has shown how elementary are both ideas, the imperial and the national alike.

If we endeavour to compare such elements in the Republic and the former Monarchy as are comparable, we observe, in the first place, that, out of the 53 million Austro-Hungarians, 20 million lived in the distinct kingdom of Hungary (including Croatia-Slavonia), and more than $1\frac{1}{2}$ million in Bosnia-Herzegovina, that 'occupied territory.' Austria, or Cisleithania, was herself so composite that the number of

Austrians did not reach one-quarter of her 30 million inhabitants. Now it is the strictly Austrian part of that State which, politically speaking, is continued by the present Republic. The Republic retains at least one-fifth of the population and one-quarter of the territory of the former Austrian State. While the area of the whole Empire was 260,000 square miles, that of Cisleithania was only 115,000 square miles. The area of the Republic is 32,369 square miles.

But neither the Dual Monarchy nor Cisleithania had any kind of homogeneity. Present-day Austria, for her part, consists, in the first place, of the Danubian districts, Upper and Lower Austria, together with the Burgenland, after which the Hungarians pine; and, in the next place, of a group of Alpine districts: the province of Salzburg on the borders of Bavaria, industrial Styria, Carinthia, whose southern part was saved at the eleventh hour, and the Tyrol, with its western extension of the Vorarlberg – which belongs entirely to the Rhine system – but with its southern part amputated.

The 'economic' area of the Republic is only nine-tenths of its total area; for in certain regions, such as the Tyrol, sterile rocks cover as much as a quarter of a province, and 42 per cent of the territory (54 per cent in Styria) consists of forest, which has a real value, but which ought to be reckoned by itself. Similarly the density of population – a little over 202 to the square mile – falls in the Tyrol to a little over 64 to the square mile. In all this, of course, there is nothing exceptional. On the other hand, what is a phenomenon in human geography perhaps unique in the world is the existence of a capital with a population of 1,865,780 souls in a

State with only 6½ million inhabitants: the grouping of one-third of the population of the country in a single urban agglomeration.

Austria's purely economic elements have nothing striking about them at first sight. The Republic possesses cornfields in Lower Austria and the Vorarlberg; potatoes in Upper Austria and the Tyrol; sugar-beet in Upper Austria, and vineyards in the hills around Vienna. Cattle-raising is first class. Agriculture has been developed in order to diminish the difficulties of livelihood; but its cost prices often exceed its sale prices. The young State has been left with some mines: the iron ore which has been worked in the mountains of Styria perhaps for the past twelve hundred years, and certainly since the thirteenth century; the copper-beds in Salzburg, which were being worked in prehistoric times; the lead-mines in Carinthia, the salt-mines in the Salzkammergut and the Tyrol, and some others; but the best coal-mines, those of Bohemia and Silesia, are now outside Austria's frontiers. Accordingly, she has succeeded in offsetting the poverty of the Styrian coal by an ingenious system of drying, and metallurgy is beginning to harness the Alpine water-power.

Austria's main trouble is that her route to a number of her traditional markets has been barred by customs barriers. Now the Empire itself lacked outlets and depended economically upon neighbouring States: its chief customers, apart from the rest of the Monarchy, were Serbia, Rumania, and the Levant. As a Danubian State, its activity tended increasingly in the direction of commerce rather than industry. A proper canal system would have made the river route from

Hamburg to the Black Sea pass by way of Vienna. Thus Vienna would have become an international centre of distribution, even more than of local consumption and production. Together with its luxury industries, it possessed all the commercial and banking organisations of a great Central European emporium. It was the economic capital of a geographical complex which was imperial, but also more and more international.

The first of the new problems which present themselves to the Republic of Austria is how to use the economic elements of a little Continental State: elements which are quite a different thing from mere debris of former Cisleithania. They include the resources of her Alpine regions, with their fine forests, their prosperous cattle-breeding, and their nascent hydro-electric industries; her natural and historical attractions, which make the tourist industry a source of profit in this hospitable, friendly land; the wealth of her fertile Danubian region and her mining and metallurgical districts.

And here is Austria's other great problem: the problem of Vienna, that international capital which compels her to be much more than a little Alpine and Upper Danubian republic. Vienna, as we knew it in the great days of the Monarchy, was able to develop only because it was a Court city and an international city. It can prosper in the future only if it is a city of trade and transit. In this case it will become one of the corner-stones of the new Austria's future prosperity.

Let us bear in mind that this city was not born by the will of any ambitious despot. Ever since the days of the

Celtic Vindobona, there has existed on the Danube, between the north-east end of the Alps and the mountains of Bohemia, at the point where the route from east to west and the route from south to north intersected, a market-place, situated at a junction first of roads and rivers, and then of railways and canals. The urban focus essential to Central Europe developed naturally on the Danube, the river which rises only fifteen miles away from the Rhine and flows across Europe all the way to the Black Sea. In addition, Vienna benefited by the fact that the Dual Monarchy established the utmost freedom of exchange over 260,000 square miles of neighbouring territory, and that, for military reasons, the two-headed Power provided the necessary capital for international commercial lines of communication.

This political Power has disappeared; but Vienna's geographical position remains the same: that position which makes the city the economic centre of attraction for all the Danubian countries. In the present-day period, Austria's economic difficulties – if we leave aside her deadly political dangers, internal as well as external – are local difficulties of adaptation, aggravated by the world crisis. This present-day period is characterised, even from the political point of view, by the fact that, while the former Austro-Hungarian complex has disappeared, the new Danubian complex is not yet organised. The Rome agreement, signed on March 17, 1934, by Italy, Austria, and Hungary, and based upon 'the complementary character of the national economic systems of the contracting parties,' has not yielded the results which were anticipated. The volume of trade between these countries has not increased; in some commodities, indeed, it has diminished. A north-south flow of trade, which would be of advantage to Italy's Adriatic ports, cannot be brought about until a steady flow of trade has first been established between Austria and the rest of the Danubian complex. If this complex developed normally – and it cannot do so until the menace of the *Anschluss* has been removed – Vienna would resume its natural rôle in it. Then a great opportunity would present itself, which the Republic of Austria would have to turn to account; for there is no such thing as geographical fatalism making the fortune of nations and States despite themselves.

If the Austrian nation proves strong enough to triumph over the Nazi danger, internal and external – that danger whose intensity was revealed to it on July 22, 1934, by the brutal murder of Chancellor Dollfuss – it may very well, at the same time, turn Austria into the type of State which, though small in area, is of great importance by reason of its position. The Republic of Austria ought to become the seat of a Continental emporium, an international centre of transit, commerce, and banking. But, apart from political dangers, the economic *sine qua non* of Austria's rebirth is that she and the States of Central and Balkan Europe should re-establish, of set purpose and on a still greater scale, that immense sphere of free commercial intercourse and exchange which was accidentally created by the States that have now disappeared.[1]

[1] Here I may recall the sensible proposal, put forward by Great Britain but rejected at the instance of Italy, which was made during the negotiation of the Treaty of Saint-Germain : that the successor-States of the Dual Monarchy should remain under a single customs régime for a period of five years.

IV

DANZIG: A TWENTIETH-CENTURY
HANSEATIC TOWN

Danzig and Poland

THE port of Danzig, on the estuary of the Vistula, that Polish river *par excellence*, is at one and the same time a German city and the natural port of Poland. But, first of all and above all else, it is a place of trade.

In the old days, people did not wear out their nerves worrying about ethnical origin or political allegiance. The big Hanseatic merchants, and the shopkeepers and workmen who depended on them, had no illusions either about the Teutonic knights, who bled Danzig as the price of the 'protection' which they imposed on it, or about the kings of Prussia, who systematically ruined the city out of spite because they were unable to lay hands on it.[1] These merchants were

[1] When Frederick II failed to obtain Danzig in 1772, he deliberately set about ruining it. The number of ships which entered the port in 1770 was 1,988. By 1782 it had fallen to 145. The year 1793 saw the beginning of the Prussian occupation, which led Schopenhauer's mother, a Danzig patrician, to declare: 'The King of Prussia fell like a vampire upon my unhappy city, which is doomed to destruction, and for years he sucked its vital juices until he exhausted it.' The appeals of the Danzigers to Holland, Great Britain, and Russia, even before the Prussian occupation; an attempt to create a Free City in 1807; the overtures of the Danzig Senate in 1813 for the city's transfer to Poland – all these were equally fruitless.

on easier terms with the Polish sovereigns, who needed the port just as the port needed their kingdom.

As a Hanseatic town, Danzig shared in the commercial monopoly which the Hanseatic league possessed in all the northern seas of Europe, from the English Channel to the Gulf of Finland. When the Turks captured Constantinople and controlled the Bosphorus, the commercial route from Eastern Europe to Northern and Western Europe ran *viâ* the Vistula. Then Danzig became the point where loads were broken and transferred from the overland or river part of the route to the sea. It played a profitable middleman's rôle.

Accordingly, Danzig's first period of greatness was that of a powerful Hanseatic town; but it soon fell under the 'protection' of the Teutonic knights. For the weakness of such commercial centres was that, even in the most glorious days of the Hanseatic league, they had to reckon with warlike princes, who were attracted by what they regarded as the fabulous wealth of these towns and lost no opportunity of squeezing their merchants. At Danzig, this part was played by the Teutonic Order, which made its appearance in the neighbourhood as early as 1225. In 1308 the Order took possession of the city, massacred part of the population, and subjected the burghers to an enforced cohabitation with them which lasted a century and a half. The knights fortified Danzig, colonised the countryside, Germanised the old Slav city, formerly known as Gdansk, and took the lion's share of the Hanseatic merchants' profits.

But geographical facts always remain the same. Under whatever régime it happens to be, Danzig is the natural port of the Vistula Basin, extending from the Carpathians to the Baltic. The tributaries of the Vistula constitute the routes of all central Poland to the national river, which takes its great bend through a region as purely Polish as it could possibly be. Nevertheless, political events may modify the relations of a port with its hinterland; and this has twice happened to Danzig.

When the Polish Republic embraced Lithuania, as well as parts of White Russia and the Ukraine, Danzig's hinterland, as Mr. Ziehm, a former president of the Danzig Senate, has pointed out, had as its eastern limits the Dvina, the Dnieper, and the Black Sea. On the other hand, the partition of Poland cut the Vistula into three sections, and the Russo-Prussian frontier separated Danzig from the greater part of its commercial sphere.

Now, in a country such as Poland, where road communication remained backward, just as railway communication still is, economic life is bound up with the river system. In the Russian part of Poland, however, the river and its tributaries were utterly neglected. The old canals, which in any case were becoming more and more inadequate, were kept in poor repair. Though the Bydgoszcz (Bromberg) canal was constructed in Prussian Poland, its object was to divert to the interior of Germany and to Stettin traffic which would normally have gone to Danzig. When Russia finally bestirred herself and undertook public works, she constructed railways which made the Polish trade currents flow to her Baltic ports. To all this was added the customs barrier between Danzig and its Russian-Polish markets. Finally, to the west the Varta

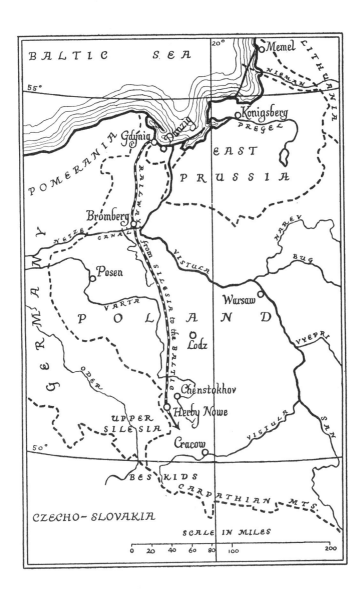

and the Netze, which flow into the Oder, carried the products of Upper Silesia and Posnania to Stettin when modern industry developed. To the east, similarly, Königsberg attracted the traffic of East Prussia. Danzig's radius of action was thus extremely restricted.

It seems, to be sure, that the some-time Free City, the old Hanseatic port of Danzig, was destined by Imperial Prussia for another rôle. Under the Hohenzollerns, Danzig became a naval base, the capital of Pomerelia, a governmental city, and a garrison town. One cannot help wondering whether it was not turned in this new direction because the Imperial Government realised that the great Hanseatic town, now that it was separated from its hinterland, could enjoy only a shadow of its former, prosperity, and that by its inclusion in the German Empire it was doomed to be nothing more than a very second-rate port.

'Remote from the main routes of international trade'; 'separated from its natural hinterland by high tariff walls'; sacrificed to its 'western rival, Stettin,' which 'invades the territory that geography itself reserves to Danzig' – this was the description which Danzig merchants gave of the city in its Chamber of Commerce Reports between 1900 and 1913. Such was Danzig on the eve of the war.

BALTIC POLAND

The southern shores of the Baltic consist for the most part of sand-dunes covered by pine-groves, varied by regions of lake or marsh. Their density of population is low, and their economic life is sluggish; for the soil, except in the delta of the Vistula, is hard to cultivate, and fishing yields poor profits. Ports have developed solely on the estuaries of the great rivers, and they are commercial centres with scarcely any territory of their own : their sphere of economic action lies in the interior, beyond the coastal provinces. Accordingly it has sufficed for these ports that they should be linked by river – or, nowadays, by railway – with their hinterland and its middle and upper basins of forestry, agriculture, mining, and industry.

For this reason, Poland is a Baltic State, though she has a very short coastline. A single seaport is enough for her. To become Baltic once more, she had only to recover that part of Pomorze (Pomerania) – a region in fact Polish – which the peace treaties gave her in order to provide her with a frontage on the sea. These few leagues of Polish coastline, which do not even embrace the estuary of the national river, doubtless do not look very much on a small-scale map : the only kind of map consulted outside specialist circles. Accordingly people have got into the habit of talking contemptuously about the 'corridor' when they refer to the Polish zone in between Prussia and the Free City of Danzig, which is so narrow that at certain points it is a passage only fifty miles wide.

Here let us digress and see how Poland has secured her access to the sea. Some historians tell us about a legendary Polish navigator who went to America with Columbus, and human geographers introduce us to Kashub fishermen. But let us study instead the posters in Polish railway stations, which for fifteen zloty – not much more than ten shillings – offer you a return ticket between Warsaw and Gdynia: a round trip of nearly two hundred leagues. They aim at making the Polish people familiar with the sea and fond of it.

Poland wanted her seaport. After the war, she demanded Danzig, her natural port; but Danzig was German, and it was refused to her. The diplomats, harking back not simply to the Middle Ages, but to the eighteenth century and the Napoleonic period, invented the Free City of Danzig. It was a possible solution, and it would probably have proved a satisfactory solution, if the only thing to take into account had been an economic arrangement between the Poles and the Danzigers. But there was a third factor: the German Reich. So the Poles doubted the security of the solution which looked so nice on the parchment of the peace treaties. They wondered whether it would be wise for them to revert to the policy of their sometime kings, and live as landsmen with the seaport of their national river system continually under threat of becoming once more part of a foreign, and perhaps hostile, State.

Moreover, if Danzig is German, the Pomorze is a Polish region: unquestionably Polish. While descendants of Frisians are to be found on the coast – for example, in the sandy Hel 'arrow' – who speak a Germanic dialect, though they sometimes bear Slav names (you find a man with a Frisian name among the leaders of the Polish party, while another man with a Polish name is known for his German sympathies), the Kashub district and what is called the 'corridor' are almost entirely Polish. Now Poles have settled at Gdynia. The swarms of children on their way to school sing and quarrel among themselves in the Polish language – and obviously they are not thinking of deceiving the foreign visitor. German pre-war statistics showed a high percentage of Polish population in this region. Now the Poles are really peopling it: they are multiplying in that quiet way of theirs which everywhere gives Polish development all the characteristics and appearance of a force of nature.

At Gdynia, out of a little fishing hamlet, Poland has created a national port. The town is on the edge of a dreary marsh district; but it stands on a bay with a sandy bottom thirty to fifty feet deep, well sheltered by one of those coastal sandy breakwaters which the Germans call *Nehrung*. In addition, the Putziger Nehrung diverts the currents so that they carry the sand out to sea and maintain a natural, permanent dredging of the entrance to the bay. Even the hardest winter does not close the port, which can always be freed by ice-breakers. These excellent maritime conditions were happily completed by a desert coast around the intended port. There was nothing but a few villas, perhaps three hundred fishermen, all told a population not much over five hundred. So the ground was free for town-planning; and it was equally easy to excavate in the peaty soil to construct docks.

The town was first planned in 1924. Within ten years the port was practically completed. Apart from the technical services of a port, the Poles have already constructed a refrigerating plant, a rice-husking plant, and an oil-mill. The fishing hamlet is now a modern town with 55,000 inhabitants. In 1931 the registered tonnage of ships entering and leaving the port exceeded 2,650,000. One-quarter of them were Swedish, 18 per cent Polish, 13 per cent German, 9½ per cent Danish, 7 per cent French, and 7 per cent American. In 1934 imports totalled 992,000 tons, and exports 6,200,000 tons, out of which 5,563,000 tons were coal and coke.

This astonishing Gdynia has sprung up just like a town in the American Far West. In between two districts of new houses, on the way from the up-to-date office buildings to the fashionable hotels facing the beach, a well-paved street, flooded with electric light, runs through the middle of a field of cabbages. Gdynia is the very antithesis of Danzig, where, if you want to grasp the city properly, you must start from its old medieval heart, the Rathaus and the Langemarkt, and make your way to the modern port. In Gdynia you must plunge into the future as you go through the town; or you may put out to sea and have a look at the docks which French engineers have constructed in the soft peat of the shore, well sheltered by the Nehrung, on which the Hel lighthouse gleams like a carbuncle on the brow of young Poland.

Is Gdynia an artificial creation with no future before it, as is alleged by certain supporters of the German, and even of the Danzig, point of view? Is it simply a costly gratification of the national vanity of a country which has not yet emerged from its period of poverty? Are not the Poles themselves somewhat uneasy about it? The territory of the Free City of Danzig occupies the fertile soil of the Vistula delta – part of it is below sea-level, and one can recognise the handiwork of the Dutch – and it constitutes a real geographical entity, not simply an arbitrary creation of diplomats. Gdynia, it is true, possesses nothing to be compared with this territory; but it is admirably situated from the maritime point of view. It is the

port of western Poland, linked by the Silesia-Baltic
railway - constructed, like Gdynia itself, by French
industry – with the coal-fields and the industrial
districts of Upper Silesia, and with Czechoslovakia
still further away. Already international connections
between the Baltic, Central Europe and the Balkans
are contemplated for the future.

THE FREE CITY OF DANZIG

If such may be the future of Gdynia, what will be
that of Danzig? Is not the dream of a modern
Hanseatic town on the estuary of the Vistula now
doomed never to come true? The present reality is
that the economic conception of Danzig, as a Free City
and the German port of the Republic of Poland, has
been stultified by political factors, by events of the same
kind as those which led to the Polish decision to construct Gdynia. But one fact remains, and it cannot
disappear overnight. That fact is the existence of
the Free City of Danzig.

The outstanding feature of Danzig's present situation is that, as a Free City, it is in complete control
of its municipal life; but it is not a Sovereign State,
and its international relations are controlled by the
Polish Government. As a commercial centre and
a port for Poland, it lives under a régime of Customs
union with Poland, and its port is administered by a
mixed Danzig-Polish commission, presided over by a
Swiss. In theory, nothing could be more logical,
not to say simple. In practice, difficulties are numerous: some of them purely political, most of them
economic manifestations of political disagreement,
a few of them entirely economic in character.

In a lecture delivered in the spring of 1933 in Paris, at the Carnegie Endowment for International Peace, Dr. Georg Cursen, an ex-President of the Supreme Court of the Free City, set forth 'Danzig's anxieties for to-day and to-morrow,' and showed how far Danzig-Polish co-operation was possible.

'The sole sphere,' he said, 'in which peaceful co-operation presented itself as not merely possible, but actually useful and advantageous to both parties, was the sphere of industry and commerce. *The Hanseatic spirit, which has remained alive in a large part of the population of the Free City, is to a great extent free from national prejudices.* Once it surpasses the limits of petty local trading, commerce requires to be free from artificial restrictions, such as customs frontiers, prohibitions against import, etc. Now for centuries past the great basin of the upper Vistula, formerly Russian territory, and even the Russian provinces bordering on the Black Sea, constituted an important part of the Danzig hinterland. . . . To preserve this hinterland, despite the separation of Danzig from Germany, was the legitimate desire of the Danzig merchants, who hoped that the fruitful development of commercial relations with Poland, favoured by the customs union, might to a certain extent make good the unfavourable effects due to the loss of the German market.'

Statistics show that this hope has been largely realised – though less largely than the Danzigers anticipated. But, once the present crisis is over, the future may prove better. In any case, it is in the economic sphere that Danzigers and Poles can best come to an understanding. The agreement of September 18,

1933, between Poland and Danzig bears witness to
this. In addition, without intending to do so, it
emphasised the Hanseatic character, so to speak, of
modern Danzig.

It was agreed, in the first place, that 'the Polish
Government and the Senate of the Free City of Danzig
undertake, for a period of one year commencing on
October 1, 1933, to ensure that a certain quantity
of merchandise, to be enumerated in a schedule to be
published later, shall pass through the port of Danzig';
and that 'if traffic diminishes in such a way that a
certain quantity of merchandise included in the list
cannot pass through the port of Danzig, the Polish
Government and the Senate of Danzig shall come to an
agreement to offset this diminution by causing other
merchandise to circulate.'

Danzig was thus granted a privilege which recalls
the conditions that the Hanseatic league imposed on
its customers. In addition, Danzig was protected
against competition by Gdynia. 'The Polish Government undertakes not to favour the port of Gdynia by
customs facilities or by special import permits.'

This agreement was calculated to give satisfaction to
Danzig merchants and encourage them to look forward
to the end of the world economic crisis without feeling
that they were placed in a position of inferiority. It
met the complaint which the Senate of Danzig made
to the League of Nations in 1930: that the Polish
State was not fully utilising Danzig's traffic capacity,
and was favouring the port of Gdynia to its detriment.

In October, 1931, the special commissioner, Count
Gravina, acting on the advice of the jurists entrusted
by the League of Nations with inquiry into the matter,

ruled that Danzig was not entitled to demand a monopoly of Poland's maritime trade, and that Poland's
right to construct and utilise a Polish port could not
be contested; but that Poland should utilise Danzig's
capacity to the full, and should not favour another
port to its detriment by preferential treatment.   The
agreement of September 1933 put this thesis of the
League of Nations into practice word for word.

Other agreements followed it.   They were of such
a nature as to lead the Moscow newspaper *Izvestia*
to describe them, in August 1934, as equivalent to 'an
economic *Anschluss* with all its advantages on the side
of Poland.'

The explanation of these agreements was that a
German-Polish pact of non-aggression, signed in
January 1934, had transformed the relations between
the Reich and the Republic of Poland.   The Hitlerian Government guaranteed the frontiers of Poland
for a period of ten years.   To all appearance, it gave
orders that, for the time being, nothing more was to be
said about Germany's claims in Upper Silesia and in
the 'corridor.'

Accordingly, the continued existence of the Free
City of Danzig seems to be assured until 1944.   For
that matter, we have only to recall how Danzig was
treated by the Berlin Government during the past
century and a half in order to realise that, in her present-day policy in connection with Danzig, Germany,
faithful in this respect to Prussian policy, has never
considered anything but her own prestige, and not
concerned herself in the least about the city's prosperity.
The result was that, when I was in Danzig at the end
of the summer of 1933, I found that all who had any

responsibility in local political circles declared that, while wishing for the restoration of the city to the Reich, they regarded such restoration as an eventuality too remote to be made the basis of immediate practical politics. At the same time, it was easy to see that this, and nothing else, was these politicians' ideal.

Danzig, as a former garrison town, a former administrative centre, includes in its population a fair number of retired German officers and officials, men of leisure, yesterday ardent partisans of the Empire, and to-day ardent partisans of the Third Reich. The Free City draws its officials from the civil service of the Reich as it now exists, and these civil servants are transferred, for example, from Königsberg to Danzig, and from Danzig to Stettin, just as they were in 1913, without any interruption in the continuity of their careers. A number of people from East Prussia and from widely different parts of Germany have settled in Danzig, practise the liberal professions there, write to the papers and take a hand in politics.

The result is that administrative and political Danzig is just as German as though there had been no war and no peace treaties for twenty years past. The Nazi newspaper *Der Danziger Vorposten* carries the motto: '*Zurück zum Reich. Gegen verträgliche Willkür.*' It could scarcely say more explicitly that it is campaigning for treaty revision.

The Government of the Free City displays its Nazi sympathies quite openly. They are symbolised by the fact that the flag of the Reich and the swastika standard are flown on either side of the city's flag over all public buildings. On the demand of the National-Socialist Party, on February 13, 1935, Herr Greiser, the President of the Senate – in other words, the chief executive – issued a proclamation dissolving the Diet on February 23 and ordering a General Election on April 7. The reason was that the Nazis, who already possessed a majority in the Diet, wanted to acquire a majority sufficient to revise the Constitution – that is to say, a two-thirds majority. But, despite an electoral campaign in which Germans from the Reich and even the German Minister for Propaganda, Doctor Goebbels, took an active part, the Nazis, though they came back with forty-four seats instead of thirty-eight out of the total of seventy-two, were not in a position to impose upon the Free City a Constitution based on the principles of the Totalitarian State.

Political views in Danzig, in short, are finely shaded. At one extreme are those who adroitly maintain that quite a tolerable *modus vivendi* could and should be arrived at, with due regard for the peace treaties; but they add in the same breath that unhappily the Poles, for their part, pay no attention to treaties. At the other extreme are those who openly work for treaty revision, the restoration of Danzig to the Reich, and the elimination of the Polish 'corridor.' They revert, in fact, to the German proposal at Versailles: that Poland should enjoy preferential rights and free zones in the German ports of Danzig and Königsberg.

The Poles have abandoned their former demand for the inclusion of Danzig in the territory of the Polish Republic; but they refuse to admit that Danzig should be German. As for the suppression of the 'corridor,' I have never met a Pole, whatever his age or his party, who was not ready to fight to the last to keep Pomorze and Gdynia in the Polish fatherland.

Such are the two opposing parties in Danzig. On both sides, economic and political factors co-exist. The only difference is that on the Danziger side they are not to be found merged in one and the same person, as they are on the Polish side. Just as old-time Danzig possessed, at one and the same time, its Hanseatic merchants absorbed in their business and its Teutonic knights leading the politics of their days, so in present-day Danzig politics are run by the Germans from East Prussia or Germany, while the Danzigers work in their offices. This is one of the causes of the complexity and apparent contradictions which exist here between politics and business, sentiment and interest.

DANZIG AND GDYNIA

Danzig strongly resented the creation of a great Polish port within a dozen miles of its own quays, when its own potential capacity for handling traffic was superior to the present activity of its own port and Gdynia put together. The foundation of Gdynia was not decided upon for purely economic reasons. Certain Polish authors declare that the port would probably never have been constructed if Danzig had become Polish territory, as was originally suggested; but that Poland considered it impossible to have no seaport within her own frontiers.

In the Free City it is claimed that the construction of Gdynia is 'responsible for Danzig's economic catastrophe.' It is true that the word 'catastrophe' scarcely comes into one's mind when one studies the aggregate figures of the port's activity, or even when one discriminates between raw material and manufactured products. Statistics show that, between 1923 and 1928, the trade of the port of Danzig rose from 1.7 to 8.6 million tons, and that, despite the world crisis, it has since stood at over 8 million tons, while the trade of other Baltic ports remained stationary at the best, or else declined. The trade of Stettin, in particular, diminished from 6 to 5 million tons, and fell to 3.79 millions in 1931. Even though the increase in the tonnage handled is mainly due to coal and timber, it seems likely that Danzig is now making rather more profit than it did before the war.

At the same time, it is obvious that Danzig is making less profit than it would make if it had a monopoly of Polish trade, such as its merchants hoped to obtain. But it is making much more profit than it would make if it once more became a German port in German territory, as certain politicians advise it to become. Sound judges, and impartial ones, believe that the maintenance of the *status quo* is the most satisfactory solution for everybody concerned; and their views more or less coincide with those of the negotiators of the peace treaties.

From the standpoint of economic geography, therefore, the question reduces itself to this: given the definite fact of the co-existence of the two ports, Danzig and Gdynia, can they co-operate to the satisfaction of everybody concerned in accordance with the conditions laid down by the League of Nations?

Gdynia conveys to the traveller a very strong impression of youthful power, thanks to its aspect of a new town in full course of development; and he is quite taken by surprise at the sight of a great port, purely Polish in its population and its activity, since he probably assumed the Poles to be a people with little or no connection with the sea.

Danzig, on the other hand, conveys, so to speak, a more gradual impression. You start with an old Hanseatic port in an archaic setting; and, as you go down the Motlau, through an almost entirely German city, you finish up at the Neufahrwasser quays, with their extremely up-to-date equipment. You are led to think of neighbouring ports, such as Antwerp and Rotterdam. You let your imagination roam about specialisation, and perhaps about separate spheres of activity. This happens to be the maritime threshold of a State with an area of some 150,000 square miles and a nation of 32 million souls.

Danzig is the port of the Vistula, the port for merchandise transported by river no less than by rail. It will derive the utmost possible advantage from its natural position as soon as the river and canal system of which it is the maritime outlet is completely organised. Gdynia, for its part, is supplied only by the railway which brings it the products of the west of Europe and the Polish part of the Oder Basin, and by the Silesia-Baltic line, the line which runs by way of Bydgoszcz into Upper Silesia. It may become the outlet for this Polish industrial region and even for Czechoslovakia, thanks to its free port, which already has a Czechoslovak section. As a port for the Western Slav plain, it may also become a great transit port between the north and the centre of Europe: the starting-point of ever faster expresses for the Carpathians and the Balkans.

In his political testament, Frederick II wrote: 'Whoever holds the estuary of the Vistula and Danzig will be more master of Poland than he who rules her.' Danzig, the old Gdansk of the Slavs, now nine-tenths Germanised, wants to remain German and so make the prophecy of the great Prussian king come true for the benefit of the descendants of the Teutonic knights and the Baltic barons. But nature is the stronger. East Prussia, now reduced to its proper valuation, is economically of little importance. 'It now seems solely the remnant of an ambitious dream,' as a French historian, Emile Bourgeois, recently put it. Königsberg, situated at the end of its '*haff*,' in between independent Lithuania and reconstituted Poland, with a hinterland where marsh and waste abound, is above all the capital of a region of forest and grazing land.

Danzig, on the contrary, despite its sulkiness, which cannot last for ever, despite its cursing of Gdynia, is witnessing its own prosperity increase step by step with the prosperity of the Polish port. If they are capable of continuing their age-old tradition and comprehending their own interests, the merchants of the old Hanseatic town will become more and more indifferent to East Prussia and Prussian Pomerania, those remnants of an outworn policy, and become more and more interested in Poland and the new Slav complex which represent their economic future.

V

BRITISH POWER FROM EGYPT TO INDIA

FROM Suez to Singapore, from the Himalayas to
Zanzibar, extend a whole series of States whose
international status varies. They are all but unknown
to the European, who realises their interdependence
all the less because they are rarely to be found assembled on the same map.

The geographical centre of these States is in the
Sea of Oman, almost midway between Cape Guarda-
fui, the extreme easterly point of Africa, and Cape
Comorin, where India comes to an end in the South.
It was here, around the seas in which the summer
monsoon takes the sailing-ships from Africa to India,
and the winter monsoon brings them back again,
that arose the medieval power of the Oriental Arabs:
a power commercial rather than political. Their
splendid capitals, which ruled not so much over land
as over sea, were strung out along the coasts of Africa,
Arabia, and Iran, as far as Basra, on the Shatt al
Arab: the lands of the *Arabian Nights*, of treasures of
art and beauty, of fine legends and barbaric customs.

Of the Arabs and the Portuguese, Great Britain is
the modern heiress, and the waves of the Indian Ocean,
above all others, are those that Britannia rules. But
now we find this power looking as though it were
crumbling. The autumn of 1932 saw independent

Iraq enter the League of Nations, and nationalist Persia, of her own free-will, annul her contract with the Anglo-Persian Oil Company, that buttress of the British Admiralty.[1] Egypt demands the removal of the last traces of British occupation in her kingdom, which was declared independent in 1922. Ever since November 1930, a conference has been sitting, year after year, to study practical ways of making the political régime of India evolve towards a kind of Dominion status.

But all this does not really mean the decline of British power in these regions, any more than the Imperial Conference of 1926 – whatever view of it may have been taken on the Continent, to which British affairs always remain a mystery – foreshadowed the break-up of the British Empire. The truth is that a long and obscure process of evolution is to-day becoming clear, with the result that it takes those who have neglected to follow it by surprise, as though it were a cataclysm.

We must note, in passing, that this process of evolution does not take the British public by surprise; but this is only because that public pays no attention to it. World-wide views, in Great Britain as in the rest of the world, have never been secreted in more than a few picked brains.

---

[1] I preserve the word 'Persian' in the historical part of this chapter, since, at the time with which it deals, it was customary in Europe to describe as 'Persia' what is now officially known as the kingdom of Iran. In conformity with this new nomenclature, since June 1935 the Anglo-Persian Oil Company has changed its name to Anglo-Iranian Oil Company; the Persian rendering of its name was always '*Sherkaté Nafté Englisva Irân.*'

The Growth of British Power around
the Indian Ocean

A very fine chapter in the life of the British Empire is being written before our eyes; but we cannot appreciate it properly if we overlook the earlier chapters, beginning with that highly coloured Elizabethan introduction when young England sowed her wild oats looking for routes to Golconda. Youth of the world, youth of mankind ! Youth intoxicated by that Indian dream which, since Alexander, was dreamt by Greeks, Arabs, Portuguese, Spaniards, Dutch, and French, and which the English were to have for centuries the rare fortune to make true !

But in the sixteenth century the route to the East by South Africa was Portuguese, and the American route was Spanish. Fishers of herring, cod, and whale, lured into boreal navigation, searched on behalf of the merchants of Bristol in the mists for a 'North-West passage,' only to find it blocked by the pack-ice of Hudson Strait. On behalf of the traders of the City of London they tried for a 'North-East passage,' again to find themselves in a blind alley of ice. This suggested an overland route by way of Muscovy, with the result that it was Englishmen who blazed the trail for the Russians along the land routes to India by way of the Iranian plateau, the oases of Turkestan, and the passes of the Hindu Kush.

But land transport was costly, it was only safe on the roads under the control of great empires, and it was slow until modern times. From the decline of the Roman Empire until the nineteenth century, the route by way of the Atlantic and the Indian Ocean remained the only one that was practicable. England came to dominate it by means of her ports of call on the coast and in the islands of the two oceans off shore from Africa; and on the west coast was born a great colony, at the Cape of Good Hope a nation, while Zanzibar was perhaps to be the first beginning of an East African State.

From Zanzibar to Surat, England took a hand with the Arab and Persian navigators, merchants, and chiefs long before the Suez route, the railway, and the aeroplane made the Red Sea and the Persian Gulf avenues to India. None who has sailed on these enchanted waters can ever feel the same again! A new political life was to begin for the Power which should become suzerain, from Malindi to Muscat and Basra, over the sultans and sheikhs whose unicellular domains, though they might be no more than a port or an island in the Persian Gulf, were of capital importance in connection with the stretch of sea between Arabia and the Malabar coast.

Then the opening of the Suez Canal still further increased the value of this part of the old sea route. You went from Europe to India no longer by way of the Atlantic Ocean, where there was room for everybody, but by way of a corridor which even a weak coastal power could close at its narrowest points: Gibraltar, Malta, the Suez Canal, Bab-el-Mandeb.

So Great Britain had to develop another department of Moslem politics in Egypt and acquire interests in Somaliland. In the interior, the Egyptian Sudan linked on to the hinterland of the coast where Vasco da Gama had set up a *padrão*. It looked like the dawn of that East African State for which the British mandate over German East Africa was to break down the barrier that separated Kenya-Uganda from the Rhodesias and Nyasaland. The dream of an East African Dominion vanished at the first contact with reality; but meanwhile British power around the Sea of Oman was strengthened.

To speak of a Moslem policy is tantamount to saying an Arab policy. The east coast of the Red Sea is the coast of the holy cities of Islam, Mecca, and Medina; of the Hedjaz, to-day ruled by the Puritan Wahhabis; of the Yemen, ruled by the Imam Yahia. Inland is Nejd, where the Wahhabi power developed, and the desert. The Hadramaut is the hinterland of Aden. It is essential for Great Britain to follow all the intrigues and all the quarrels of sheikhs and tribes, even those which roam around the Rob' al Khali, as far as Oman and the Persian Gulf.

As though Fate, which is certainly very strong in Moslem lands, were bent on pinning down a large part of British power here, the most modern routes to India, those of the railway and the aeroplane, will converge at the head of the Persian Gulf, thence follow the Arabian coast if the Iranian coast is not available, and aim at the oil-wells – the source of the petrol that is also the life-blood of the transport.

When the Bagdad Railway was undertaken by the Germans, a direct threat was levelled at Great Britain. A rival Power was proposing to open the land route to the Persian Gulf and India. This was why, in the European war, the Mesopotamian front possessed an importance for Great Britain which was unintelligible to the man in the street. This was why Great Britain required a mandated territory in Syria stretching south-west to Egypt and south-east to the railway line to Bagdad. So, under British tutelage, the State of Iraq was formed out of three riverain *vilayets*, Mosul, Bagdad, and Basra, and desert zones with no definite frontiers. Then the value of Iraq was increased a hundred-fold by the discovery of oil on the mountainous Assyrian border, where Kirkuk is becoming a new centre of life and the head of pipe-lines to the Mediterranean coast.

But the route to India by way of Baluchistan at first followed the Iranian coast. The Iranian coast ! – the phrase evokes the whole past of the Gulf, the whole western policy of the Indian Empire; and perhaps its whole future. This burning coast is dotted, far apart, with time-honoured ports of call, whose local chieftains lived at the beginning of the twentieth century just as they did in the time of Haroun al Rashid. The Khadjar dynasty had become Teherani Merovingians and ceased to exercise any authority over them. British agents influenced these petty potentates just as their ancestors three centuries ago influenced the Indian nabobs. Yonder, on the frontier, to the north of the Shatt al Arab, at Muhamrah, ruled a sheikh who seemed to have stepped out of a medieval miniature. He was given a subsidy by the British Government. On this man's land were rich oil-wells. If war came, the Anglo-Persian Oil Company would supply British warships with fuel and make possible a watch on the Sea of Oman and the guarding of the coasts of India.

When peace was signed in 1920, the British land-route to India was assured by the Syrian mandate, the States of Palestine and Trans-Jordan, Iraq under mandate, Arabistan with its oil, and bases on the Persian Gulf and the Arabian coast. The railway, supplemented by motor-routes from the Mediterranean to the Euphrates; aeroplanes on the Bagdad service, and ships in the Persian Gulf could all operate in conjunction and complement one another.

Meanwhile India itself has attained the geographical completion of its entity. Slowly its frontier moved from the desert of Thar to the banks of the Indus, and thence to the slopes of the Hindu Kush and the Suleiman mountains. The frontier 'marches' are organised from the pass of Chitral to the coast road. To the north are the mountains: to the south is British ascendancy over Baluchistan.

Thus the Indian Empire is protected to the west by a geographical and political complex of wonderful variety and wealth: and this complex in fact embraces all the seas and lands that enchanted the Arabs before the Europeans. But it is in a ceaseless state of transformation. No sooner does Great Britain round off her achievement than one of its constituent elements is undermined so to speak, and has to be constituted all over again. History repeats itself: it never seems to have been within the power of any human strength to set up in this region a single, permanent, immutable authority, such as the well-fed, sleepy Europeans of the dawn of the twentieth century supposed their empires to be.

THE EVOLUTION OF THE ISLAMIC LANDS AND ARABIA

The Moslem world has manifested in the twentieth century a dynamic strength which had appeared to be exhausted before the dawn of modern times. The

Young Turk revolution, Egyptian nationalism, Persian constitutionalism, even the fruitless attempt to westernise Afghanistan, have all borne witness to the creation, or the rebirth, of the nationalist spirit. The last days of Hamidian Turkey saw what might have been mistaken for a revival of traditionalism and religious faith; but this was no more than an attempt to save a crumbling empire – a desperate attempt whose failure could sadden nobody but a few European dilettantes. The dead buried the dead.

But what Westerners had failed to take into account was that these new nationalisms must necessarily be xenophobe, at least to the extent that they were bound to react against the privileges which the old Islamic States had generously granted to Christians settled in their territory. The young founders of national States could not tolerate the concessions allowed by degenerate dynasties or their vassals, who were indifferent, if not hostile, to the setting-up of a strong centralised authority. One can only be astonished at the scandalised surprise of the West when the peoples of the East, emancipated by Western teaching, showed themselves just as unfavourable to foreign schools, missions, and establishments of all kinds as the reactionary pashas of the old days had been indulgent towards European consuls, merchants, and monks.

The treaties whose prototype was the 'Capitulations' negotiated between Francis I of France and Sultan Suleiman have become obsolete. They would, indeed, have had to be remarkably well constructed, and the East would have had to remain remarkably immobile, if these conventions were to continue operative after a lapse of four centuries. That does not alter the fact that fresh ones have to be drawn up on a new basis.

British diplomacy has problems of this kind to solve throughout its Moslem sphere. But it is particularly well equipped for such changes; for it is richer in tradition than in doctrine, and it is endowed with that faculty of adaptability to circumstances which gives British institutions, for all their apparent conservatism, so much suppleness.

It so happens that no diplomacy is more directly in contact than British diplomacy with the fundamental problem of Islam. That problem is Arabia.

It is a problem all the more complex because it is religious as much as political, and all the more delicate because it is religious before it is political. Geographically it is the stiffest of problems because it extends to the lands of all the tribes and States of Arabia and concerns the frontiers of Egypt, Syria, Trans-Jordan, and Iraq, and also the maritime frontiers of the Red Sea, the Indian Ocean, and the Persian Gulf. Arabia is situated in the centre of the Moslem world, and its influence radiates far beyond its own geographical sphere.

A kind of unity has been created in Arabia by the Wahhabite domination of the Saud family. Since the leader of the 'Puritans of Islam' expelled the family of the Grand Sherif of Mecca from the holy cities, the Hedjaz and Nejd, united under the name of Saudi Arabia or Saudieh, form a single State, with two capitals, Mecca in the Hedjaz and Riyadh in Nejd; and since 1928 Asir has also been under the domination of Ibn Saud. But strong British footholds dot the coasts, where the Sultan of Oman, the Sheikh of Koweit,

the Emir of the Bahrein Islands, and the chieftains
of the Pirate coast and Hadramaut are protected by
Great Britain, subsidised by her, and allied with her.
Aden is a British base.   Only indomitable, mountainous Yemen remains independent.

The activity of Great Britain in this Arab world
is a matter for marvelling.   Everywhere her agents,
official and unofficial, are at work.   Their shrewdness
has never found better expression than it did in their
adaptability to the transformation in the Hedjaz.

The Grand Sherif of Mecca had signed a treaty with
Great Britain, in 1922, which was tantamount to the
establishment of a British protectorate, in return for
an annual subsidy of £400,000 – which led him to lose
the confidence of the Moslem world.   Then, within
a few years, the Wahhabite *malik* Abdul Aziz ibn Saud
conquered the interior of the peninsula, and came in
contact in the north with the frontiers of Syria and
Iraq, where seasonal movements of tribes on the war-
path periodically disturbed the peace.   He proceeded
to expel the Hashimite family from Mecca, where he
was proclaimed king on January 8, 1926.   On May
29, 1927, Great Britain signed a treaty with him where-
by she recognised the complete independence of the
Kingdom of Arabia.   Then she went on to secure
for herself a preponderant influence in Ibn Saud's
counsels in economic matters and in his relations with
the protected coastal States, and with Trans-Jordan
and Iraq, which were also ruled by British *protégés:*
none other than the son and the grandson of the
Hashimite Grand Sherif, the British vassal whom Ibn
Saud had expelled from Mecca.

Meanwhile another form of Britain's activity in

Arabia yields nothing to her political activity. This other form is scientific exploration.

The Southern desert, the Rob' al Khali (the 'Empty Quarter') had remained the most mysterious of deserts. No European, and perhaps nobody at all, had ever completely crossed it. In December 1930 and January 1931, Mr. Bertram Thomas, the very type of Britain's excellent agents in the Persian Gulf region, who had been successively an official in Mesopotamia, and then counsellor first to the Emir of Trans-Jordan and next to the Sultan of Muscat, crossed this desert from Dhofar on the Sea of Oman to the peninsula of Qatar on the Persian Gulf, picking up the possible tracks of biblical caravans and discovering a hitherto unknown lake seven miles long by a mile and a half wide. Exactly a year later, Mr. H. St. John Philby, an English Moslem, counsellor to Ibn Saud, carried out a fine piece of exploration in the centre and west of the Rob' al Khali, in the course of which he found that the legendary site where the Arabs place the ruins of Ophir, destroyed by fire from Heaven, is a landscape of craters created by gigantic meteorites.

Side by side with these Arabised Englishmen, we find that Oxford don who became Colonel Lawrence, and died in 1935, so tragically alone. We find the late Gertrude Bell, greatly regretted, who died from overwork in Bagdad in July 1926, and who wrote: 'It's shocking how the East has wound itself round my heart till I don't know which is me and which is it.' We find Sir Andrew Ryan, the British envoy at Riyadh. Apart from them, there are agents of the British Empire, too many to mention, who make the Arab world a political complex which is as much British

as Moslem in its inspiration. All these agents work
with the same enthusiasm, down to the humblest of
them, like those worthy clerks at Perim – according
to a ballad which appeared in *Punch* on October 19,
1932 –

> Who dwell in this smitten
> And waterless hole,
> For the sake of Great Britain,
> Her cables and coal.

'It is essential,' Miss Bell wrote, 'that India and
Egypt should keep in the closest touch, since they are
dealing with two sides of the same problem.' Great
Britain's Arab policy is the guardian of the Indian
Empire. Every political event, however local it may
appear, reverberates in successive echoes from the Red
Sea to Burma. The Red Sea, moreover, has two sides.
Opposite the Arab side is the Egyptian side. The
Moslem British Empire has for its normal western
boundary the Libyan desert.

EGYPTIAN NATIONALISM

Egypt is a territory where for thousands of years
foreign dominations of all kinds and all origins have
succeeded one another. She owes this apparently surprising return of a situation which perpetually repeats
itself to the fact that she is crossed by an international
route. This route is indispensable to the British
Empire, and it cannot be left entirely outside the
control of that Empire.

To the *fellah*, little it matters who governs, from the
Pharaoh to the Greek, from the Osmanli or the Egyptian, to the British. Egyptian nationalism is not a mass
opinion. Nevertheless, given the composite ethnical

elements in Egypt, it may very well be a power, and so it has proved.

The British occupation in Egypt, for its part, has been a corollary of the Suez Canal since 1869, and also of the Egyptian Sudan since about 1880. Nothing could be more different from sentimental nationalism, nothing could be more opposed to it, more of an antithesis to it, than this rational, realist policy. Whether the British have administered Egypt well or ill, little the Egyptians care. In the success of this foreign effort to put the Egyptian house in order – as it has been since 1900 – the nationalists find only one reason the more for bidding the foreigners begone from a country which thinks it no longer needs them.

Persistent, too, has been the legacy of mistakes and blunders: of the violence which old soldiers everywhere think to be a cure for revolt; of the weakness which leads politicians of the Left to offer advice with all the impetuosity of philanthropists who do not trouble themselves about hard facts. In the upshot, in 1922, Great Britain recognised Egypt as an independent kingdom. Just as she later recognised Iraq? Not at all. It was quite a different thing – though Great Britain may have learned in Cairo the lesson which she applied in Bagdad. Having recognised Egyptian independence because she could not do anything else, she prepared Iraq for receiving her freedom when nothing constrained her to give Iraq that freedom.

In Egypt independence had to be restricted in order to reserve 'the vital rights and interests of Great Britain': those rights and interests 'which His Majesty's Government cannot admit should be called into question or discussed by any other Power.' Hence the maintenance of the Capitulations; the maintenance of British garrisons – some 11,000 men in all – in Cairo, in Alexandria, and along the Canal; and the maintenance of British domination in the Egyptian Sudan.

Let us leave aside the Capitulations, which concern all foreigners. As for the Sudan, Egypt claims it as her waterworks. On the other hand, the agricultural system of the Nile valley is such that the water-tap is also, so to speak, the larder-key. Further, Gordon's Sudan, ransomed by British blood, represents an essentially British achievement. It is difficult to imagine Great Britain surrendering the Egyptian Sudan to another Power or to some new Mahdi, especially at a time when Uganda and Kenya are being developed so rapidly. Since 1934, Italy's policy in Ethiopia has made it more than ever essential that the Sudan should be under the control of a strong Power, capable of keeping an eye on Lake Tana, together with the rivers Bahr-el-Azrek, Atbara and Sobat, and so safeguarding the sources of the Nile in the Abyssinian highlands.

But to-day the main British question in Egypt is the guardianship of the Suez Canal, which, as Bismarck put it, links 'the Western half and the Eastern half of the British Empire just as the cervical nerve links the spinal column to the brain.' For that matter, the British right to keep an eye on the Canal is not contested in Cairo, where it is only demanded that the British troops should be withdrawn from the capital and from Alexandria.

The controversy will hinge upon the question whether it suffices for the British troops to occupy a 'canal zone,' or whether the guardianship of the canal implies the defence of the whole of Egypt; for the Canal would be put in great peril if Egypt were occupied by a hostile army, whether it were foreign or even Egyptian.

So we come back to the policy of the route to India and Australia: the sea-route by way of Suez; the land-route and the air-route by way of Palestine, Iraq, and the Persian Gulf, where will be situated the halts for aeroplanes flying from London to Karachi.

IRAQ

Iraq presents a strange chapter – but strange only in appearance – in political geography.

Here is a State with heterogeneous territory, with variable and, so to speak, fluid frontiers, which conveys the impression that it is the fruit of the will of men, and even of foreigners, just as though nature had next to nothing to do with it. But analysis of the history of Mesopotamia demonstrates the rôle of geographical factors.

In the first place, there is the route – and what a route ! It is the route from the West to India and the East, at once the most ancient and the most modern; for in the twentieth century the Syro-Mesopotamian isthmus is once more the road to India; and the aeroplane, following the line of tracks and valleys, gives new life to the land-route instead of consigning it to oblivion. Here history goes back more than fifty centuries, and we get the impression that we are bending over one of the cradles of the human race.

A fertile land, bearing two crops a year, strung out between deserts like another Egypt, Mesopotamia with her wealth has always attracted pillaging nomads; but the activity of traffic towards the Shiite holy cities,

Kerbela and Nedjef, has been a safeguard to her. Let us go back only to the seventh century. With the Arab conquest began six hundred years of that refined civilisation about which the very name of Bagdad sets us dreaming. But in the thirteenth century came Hulaku Khan's Mongols, who destroyed even the irrigation channels. Since then, despite the Turkish conquest by Suleiman the Magnificent in 1573, Iraq did not again emerge from lethargy amid her ruins until the time of Western penetration in the twentieth century.

A zone where the Turkish world and the Arab world meet – the language frontier runs from Antioch to Mosul, and then along the mountains east of the Tigris to the Diala in the south – Iraq is one of the lands where, just the same as in its understandings with the chieftains of the Persian Gulf, British policy defended the western 'marches' of India by leaning upon the Arab elements. Accordingly, in the last war, von der Goltz, the leader of the Turkish 6th Army, dreamed of forming a Turco-Irano-Afghan confederation against India; while from Basra the British moved up the valleys of the Tigris and the Euphrates, revictualling the riverain *vilayets*, and organising them through members of the Indian civil service.

In a declaration dated November 7, 1918, the British and French Governments set on record that they aimed at 'the complete and definitive freeing of the peoples so long oppressed by the Turks, and the establishment of national Governments, deriving their authority from the free choice of the native populations.' Exciting days followed. Finally the League of Nations gave Great Britain a mandate for Iraq; and, as no native

leader was to be found, the Emir Feisal was crowned
King of Iraq on August 23, 1931.   Henceforth Great
Britain was a fairy godmother to the young State.

It was not enough to create the Kingdom of Iraq : its
territory had to be determined and its frontiers had to
be fixed.   The traditional nucleus of the State consists
of the three *vilayets* strung out along the river – Basra,
Bagdad, and Mosul.   As early as 1908, irrigation works
directed by Sir William Willcocks had begun to pave
the way for a new life for Lower and Middle Mesopotamia.   Wherever the water reaches, two crops a year
are now reaped : wheat, barley, rice, maize, and beans.
The cotton crop will yield 300,000 bales a year.   Iraqi
dates are already popular in Great Britain.   Later
something will be said about the country's wealth in
oil.   In the northern mountains water-power, even in
the dry season, could develop 500,000 h.p. – not to
speak of the Tigris and the Euphrates.   But capital is
still shy.

So there has been constituted a modern political
unit which is geographically coherent.   It is to be
noticed that it is not the same as the political units,
which were also geographically coherent, in the days
of the ancient Chaldeans, the warriors of Nineveh, the
builders of Babylon, or the Arab Caliphs ; for, if their
achievements succeeded one another on the same
ground, men changed with the centuries and their
labour modified even their physical environment.   Iraq
does not reproduce any of the ancient empires on the
map.   Physically it does not correspond with the
natural region of the Mesopotamian rivers.   Nevertheless, it may be regarded as defined by the parallel
valleys and their routes – water-routes in the case of the

Tigris, land-routes rather in the case of the Euphrates – around which crystallise the irrigated land, the oil region, and the region of water-power.

If Iraq remains a peaceful, prosperous centre, its power of attraction will gradually grow.   It will attach to itself the desert regions, the frontier zones which gradually shade off until they merge into those of the neighbouring countries.   More and more firmly will there be stamped upon the map the figure of this State, a British political creation, but a natural revival of the empires of long ago.

Its king, Feisal, descendant of Fatima, daughter of Mahomet the Prophet of Allah, made it one cornerstone of the Arab confederation of which he dreamed. The other three were his native Hedjaz, Trans-Jordan, ruled by his younger brother, and Syria, where he himself in 1926 received, at Damascus, an ephemeral crown.   But Feisal died suddenly in September 1933, leaving a sovereign of twenty to reign over Iraq, whose childish nationalism had such great need to be tempered by the practical spirit of an experienced prince.

Since October 4, 1932, Iraq has been a member of the League of Nations, through the initiative of Great Britain, the very Power that created and organised her. All links between her and the mother-Power are broken. Yet Iraqi nationalism does not show Great Britain the least gratitude for having thus endowed its country. The reason is that it is not in a position to understand the operation of political synthesis – one of the boldest of our time – from which Iraq has sprung full-grown. Left to itself, the young State has begun by using its strength almost against itself.   It has aroused world-opinion against it by massacring the Assyro-Chaldeans.

Meanwhile British travellers smile when they hear the Bagdad Government say that there is no further need for the protection of the British Air Force, while the tribal chiefs ask them when the British aeroplanes are going away, so that they may revert to the fruitful pillaging of the good old days.

That is why Iraq remains a pawn in Great Britain's hands on the Arab political chess-board.

THE OIL OF IRAQ

If the northern frontier of Iraq proved difficult to delimit, the cause was not so much uncertainty about the natural territory of the new nation, or difficulties with the Kurdish and Armenian populations and with those Assyro-Chaldeans whose fate was to prove so tragic. It was rather European rivalries over an oil-bearing region where, for the past twelve years, economic interests had been coming to the fore.

The oil region begins at the north in the Caucasus and extends to the east of the Tigris, in the tertiary deposits in the mountainous country bordering on the Iranian plateau, from the Armenian Taurus into Persia. In Iraq, the richest part of it is between the Great Zab and the Diala, with Kirkuk as its centre. The Persian wells succeed one another at the foot of the Zagros mountains, then in Kurdistan and Arabistan, and finally, further to the east, on the north coast of the Persian Gulf in the island of Kishm in the neighbourhood of Bandar Abbas.

On the pre-war political map, the part of the oil region now Iraqi was within the Turkish Empire, which gave a concession for the wells to Germans connected with the Deutsche Bank and the Bagdad Railway. In

Persia a New Zealander, with the Norman-Irish name of d'Arcy, obtained, in 1901, a concession to exploit for a period of sixty years all the wells in the country, with the exception of the five northern provinces, Azerbaijan, Gilan, Mazanderan, Astrabad, and Khorassan, which were reserved to Russia.   But the territory conceded was still twice the size of France. Its exploitation dates from the formation of the Anglo-Persian Oil Company in 1909.   Finally, in 1912, the Turkish Petroleum Company was formed for the exploitation of the wells in Iraq.   An understanding was reached with the Bakhtiari, those warrior tribesmen who would have pillaged the wells but for the happy idea of making them guardians.

As soon as the war had made the dismemberment of the Turkish Empire a certainty, spheres of influence were projected in Mesopotamia and Persia: a Russian zone in the north, and a British zone in the south, with a central French zone.   This zone covered the *vilayet* of Mosul, in which the rights created by earlier concessions were maintained.   Prolonged negotiations followed, in which Dutch and American groups took part.   France acquired the German share in the Turkish Petroleum Company, then 20 per cent of the oil in Iraq, when she was confronted with the young State placed under British mandate.   An agreement, signed on March 14, 1925, between the Turkish Petroleum Company and Iraq, put all the oil in the *vilayets* of Mosul and Bagdad within the sphere of the company.   Then the League of Nations proceeded to draw the 'Brussels line' in the north of the kingdom as the Turco-Iraqi frontier, giving the oil area to Iraq and financial compensation to the Turkish Republic.

It remained to settle the itinerary of the pipe-line which would take the oil to the Mediterranean.

The mandates had divided the region concerned between France to the north and Great Britain to the

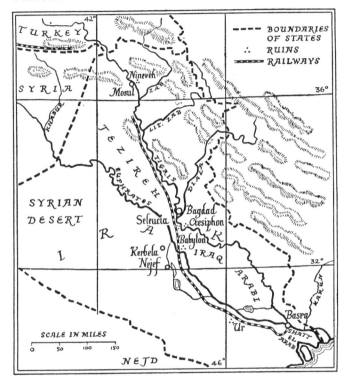

south and east. In whose territory was the pipe-line, leading from the Kirkuk district to the sea, to be constructed? There was no question about the first part of it. It would cross the Djebel Hamrin by the Fatah pass and reach the Euphrates at Haditha. After that, however, its course would depend not so much on the lie of the land as on the political map.

The Iraq Petroleum Company, which includes American, British, French, and Dutch interests, preferred, for technical and commercial reasons, a route which ran *viâ* Palmyra in a straight line to Tripolis. This was the most direct and the least expensive way. At the same time, it led from the Euphrates through territory under French mandate. So France found that nature and industrial requirements were both alike in her favour; for the ending of the Iraqi pipe-line at a French port is of first-class value not only for the national defence of France, but also for her economic life. On the other hand, Iraq, Trans-Jordan and Palestine wanted the pipe-line to run to Haifa, in the belief that it would some day be coupled with a railway, which would be of value for the development of their territory; and the British Admiralty insisted that the pipe-line should end at a British port.

A compromise was reached by the Iraq Petroleum Company, and ratified by the Iraqi Parliament, which satisfied both these seemingly irreconcilable points of view. The pipe-line, which was inaugurated at Kirkuk on January 14, 1935, by King Ghazi of Iraq, takes the form of a 'Y.' It is single from Kirkuk to Haditha, but after crossing the Euphrates it bifurcates. The northern branch runs on to Palmyra and Homs, whence it turns south-west; it continues through the Lebanon, and reaches the sea at Tripolis. The southern branch runs to the Rutba wells, thence follows the frontier, and reaches the sea at Haifa.

This double pipe-line, seven hundred and fifty miles

long, cost at least £10,000,000. Eleven pumping-stations have been established along its route, and are supplied with water through long conduits laid across the desert. Alongside the pipe-line runs a telegraph-line. There are also wireless telegraph stations, and a police force, organised by the Iraqi, Trans-Jordanian, British, and French Governments in collaboration, patrols the pipe-line and protects it against attack by the desert Bedouin.

To the young kingdom of Iraq this oil is an inexhaustible source of wealth. Its permanence has been assured to it by the grant to the Iraq Petroleum Company of a concession for seventy years, dating from 1925: a concession which incidentally guarantees the company exploitation of any wells discovered by it to the east of the Tigris. Thanks to the revenue from this concession, Iraq, in the midst of a world suffering from the longest and most acute economic crisis ever known, has been able to undertake a Five Years' Plan involving an expenditure of £800,000 a year. This will be devoted to the construction of means of communication and an irrigation system, which will restore the soil of Mesopotamia to its ancient fruitfulness. Unfortunately, however, while Iraq is thus sheltered from the economic crisis, she suffers from political crises, which set the professional politicians of the towns at odds with the representatives of the tribes, and private interests at odds with the interests of the country.

MAIDAN-I-NAFTUN AND PERSIAN GULF POLITICS

The old Persian Government, on the contrary, had not managed to make much out of the Anglo-Persian

Oil Company. The d'Arcy concession conceded it only 16 per cent of the company's net profits. On account of the economic crisis, production was deliberately reduced to six or seven million tons. Out of fifty wells bored, only twelve were being worked.

The result was that in 1932 Persia demanded a revision of the contract from the British Government, which holds half the company's shares. Jurists were all ready to denounce Persia's action as unilateral modification of a reciprocal agreement. Before the dispute even came before the League of Nations, however, it was settled out of court; for the London Government, no less than the Teheran Government, realised that the contract must be redrafted on a new basis.

This was an international event highly characteristic of our time; and it is worth while to trace it back to its origins – all the more so because it really concerned Anglo-Persian relations as a whole, and marked an important phase in the evolution of British policy in the Persian Gulf.

The fifty wells to-day connected with the great pipeline which takes their oil to the refinery at Abadan are almost all in the Maidan-i-Naftun (the 'Valley of Oil.') In other words, only one district – the largest and the most productive district, it is true – in the southern Persian oil area is at present being worked.

This oil region, bounded by the Karun, the Bakhtiari mountains, the valley of the Kerkha, and the Persian Gulf, is situated in Khuzistan and Persian Arabistan, where Arabs and Iranians meet and mingle. It shared in the great Sassanid civilisation, whose remains give so much originality to Shuster, which was xenophobe and refractory to later innovations. It was once Elam

and Susiana; and the ruins of Susa, on the right bank
of the Kerkha, queen it among all the matchless ruins
of Persia. The soil of Arabistan, made fruitful by
vanished generations, has become a quasi-desert, where
nomad, poverty-stricken shepherds roam a once fertile
land.

Following the course of the Karun or the Kerkha,
you reach the Shatt al Arab. You come to Muhamrah, ruled only the other day by a sheikh who
seemed to have stepped out of a chapter of the *Arabian
Nights*; to Basra and to the Persian Gulf, with its ports
where Sinbad the Sailor might still not be out of his
element even to-day, and where he would certainly
have found himself quite at home at the beginning of
the century.

Between the mountains and the sea the Karun makes
a great curve, and this curve surrounds the Valley of
Oil. Here is the great centre of extraction, now called
Masjid-i-Suleiman, on account of the ruins of a temple.
In the eyes of the natives, any ruined temple could
have been built by Solomon. In fact, it was a fire
temple, where, perhaps fifty centuries ago, already
burnt the mysterious sacred flame, which seemingly
was never given any fuel and was really fed by a sub-
terranean conduit, whose secret was known only to
the high priest.

Further to the south, Ahwaz, the old city on the
Karun visited by Alexander the Great, now a village
of mud huts, is supplemented by a modern British
town, where the engineers and overseers in charge of
the work on the oil-wells may have some illusion that
they are in England. It is these engineers and overseers who have filled the Maidan-i-Naftun with derricks

and constructed a railway and the pipe-lines which take the oil one hundred and fifty miles south to the island of Abadan, surrounded by an arm of the river. Here is the refinery, which employs 7,000 workmen: a European factory reproduced under one of the most burning skies, and on one of the most dismal coasts, of Asia.

This land, once belonging to the great empires of antiquity, has undergone an evolution – or rather suffered a process of political dissolution – parallel with its economic and demographic decadence. The name of Arabistan indicates that Semitic tribes – most of them Shiites like the Iranians – settled here. The ports and their neighbourhood were under the authority of sheikhs whose wealth, like their ways, made the days of legend survive into our own time.

Such a man is the now octogenarian sheikh of Muhamrah, the immensely rich Sir Khazal Khan, lord of the oil-fields, who was allied with Great Britain and subsidised by her, and was later to be held at Teheran in a gilded captivity. At a time when his blood ran more hotly in his veins, Khazal Khan was seized with desire for a girl beloved by his vizier. Since he did not want either to get rid of a useful servant or to forego satisfying his jealousy, the sheikh had an idea. He presented a magnificent casket to the vizier, and said to him: 'It is my pleasure to give you what you most desire. Take this casket in remembrance of me.' When the vizier got home and opened the casket, he found inside it the freshly cut-off head of the beautiful girl who had had the misfortune to be beloved by both servant and master. Around the Persian Gulf, a

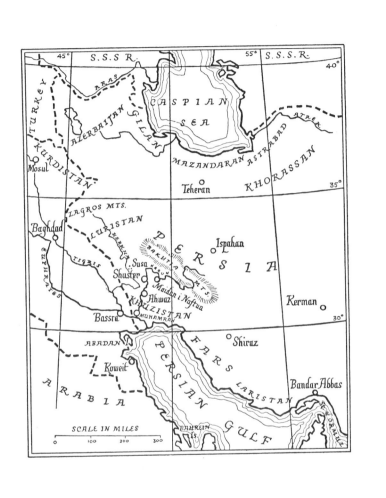

human lifetime suffices to stretch from such an adventure of the barbarous ages to modern competition for
oil wealth and control of the air route to India.

The evolution of power in this area has been no less
striking.   At the time when the weak Khadjar Shah
of Persia, Muzaffer-ed-din, yielded all the naphtha
wells of Iran to a New Zealand prospector, the sheikh
of Muhamrah, *de facto* sovereign of Arabistan and
Khuzistan, was able to treat on his own account with
the European Power which ruled the waves of the Gulf.
In 1919 Great Britain, which five years earlier had had
to share the oil-fields of Mesopotamia with a German
bank and a Dutch oil-group, was in a position to take
under her protection all the wells from the Persian
Gulf to the Caucasus, and to create a North Persian
Oil Company to exploit the former Russian zone.
Furthermore, the treaty of August 9 of the same year
entrusted British engineers with responsibility for
developing Persia, and British police officers with
responsibility for preserving order in the country.

It so happened, however, that Soviet Russia pursued
precisely the same imperialist policy which had been
followed by the Tsars, from Ivan the Terrible and
Peter the Great down to the last of the Romanoffs.
Meanwhile Persia developed a nationalist movement
which was to issue in Riza Khan Pahlevi's policy of
independence.   Russia recovered her oil-fields, and
the concession to the North Persian Oil Company was
cancelled.   In 1927 Persia abolished the Capitulations
and disbanded the *gendarmerie* commanded by British
officers in the south.

Here was the route to India barred.   Imperial Airways was unable to obtain landing-grounds in Persia.

Its planes had to follow the Arabian coast of the Gulf. Russia took up again her old project of a trans-Persian railway from the Caucasus to a port to be established on the Gulf. Next it was the turn of the southern oil-fields. Great Britain washed her hands of her old ally, Sir Khazal Khan of Muhamrah, and he was imprisoned at Teheran – a warning to the Gulf chieftains against compromising the integrity of Persian territory; and the concession to the Anglo-Persian Oil Company was cancelled.

The reason of all this was that Persia had become a nationalist State. Her sovereign did not propose to alienate any scrap of the State territory, or – as the abolition of the Capitulations bore witness – any part of his own authority. Riza Khan did not forget that he had been raised to the throne to defend Persia's independence: her economic no less than her political independence.

It has been claimed that to this factor must be added Soviet intrigue and also intrigue by American oil interests. But the disgrace of Teymurtash Khan in December 1932 indicated a weakening of Russian influence. For the rest, times have changed in Persia not only for Great Britain, but also for the various influences opposed to hers. Those influences cannot now work as they did twenty-five years ago. In that period, between the Russian zone to the north and the British zone to the south, Teheran, just like the local chieftains, concerned itself simply with raking in plenty of *bakshish* from both sides and left the foreigners to reap their harvest. In the first flush of the enthusiasm engendered by the rebirth of nationalism, it became Persia's ideal to eliminate all foreigners, except for a

handful of indispensable technical experts. Rosita
Forbes, the Scottish explorer of Moslem lands, relates
that, in the summer of 1932, the Shah told her that
this process of elimination would be accomplished by
1934.

Meanwhile, however, economic agreement for exploitation of Iran's oil was reached through the Council
of the League of Nations in October 1933, and since
then the Government and the company have colla-
borated cordially in measures for the development and
modernisation of the south of the country. From the
political point of view, British diplomats have since
had an opportunity to show whether they are as capable
as their predecessors of adapting themselves to new
conditions: a nationalist Iran and forms of Russian
and American influence different from those of the
past. It might not be a bad thing for them to re-read
the records of the foreign advisers of a score of years
ago: a fuel-supply for the fleet, and landing-grounds
on the air-route to India are well worth the effort.
Doubtless the deplorable formula will often be repeated
in London that what is needed is imagination. What
is really needed is understanding. An Iran with her
nationalist spirit awakened is rising on the Eastern
horizon. Her foreign policy will be mainly conditioned
by the attitude adopted towards her by Europe, and,
above all, by Great Britain.

The faculty of adaptation possessed by British power
was demonstrated in April 1935 by the transfer of the
naval stations on the Persian Gulf. Basaidu on Kishm
island and the neighbouring islet of Hanjam have been
abandoned by the British Admiralty in favour of the
Bahrein islands. The Imperial Airways route from

Karachi leaves the Iranian coast at Gwadar, whence it runs straight to the Bahreins. These islands are rich in oil, and one of them, Muharraq, possesses the finest natural aerodrome between England and India.

Thus the most recent history of the countries around the Gulf shows that here, at least, any such tragedy for the world will be avoided as would result from failure by Westerners to realise that treaties are no longer to be made in the East in the same way as they were at the time of Vasco da Gama's voyages, or even at the time of William Knox d'Arcy's prospecting and the adventures of the American adviser, Mr. Morgan Shuster.

INDIA: AN IMPERIAL CENTRE IN THE BRITISH EMPIRE

In India a similar tragedy would be the tragedy not only of British domination, but also of the Indian traditional organisation – a grim tragedy in this Asia where the awakening nations proclaim, in the same breath, their duty to be themselves and a curious ambition to imitate the West.

The sessions of the Indian Round Table Conference have demonstrated that various ways may lead to the establishment of modern States in certain Oriental countries. For such is, in fact, the problem to be solved. It is ridiculous to represent the Anglo-Indian difficulties as the struggle of a nation against its oppressor. India, made up of so many States, peoples, and religions, has never been able to form an empire of her own. She has always required some foreign authority, such as that of the Great Mogul or that of Great Britain.

To-day a federation between the provinces under

British administration and the self-governing States has become conceivable. But who could contemplate the task of uniting Hindus and Moslems, Brahmins, Kshatriyas, Vaisyas, Sudras, and Pariahs, men of the Punjab and the Deccan, of Orissa and Gujarat, in one and the same State under a common Constitution ? Must it not be taken for granted that these elements can form a free State and govern themselves only if the initial organisation comes from outside, and that India is impotent to '*fara da se*' in freedom no less than in subjection ?

At every turn of the road there is need for a guide who can foresee the smallest obstacles, and who is wise enough not to let himself be led astray by even the most attractive visions. For example, to embody in a Constitution protective measures for the Pariahs and for minorities – Moslems among the Hindus, Hindus among the Moslems – would be tantamount to stereotyping religious hatred and caste organisation; whereas, on the contrary, these must gradually be smoothed away until they disappear.

A Constitution for India is probably not a reality of to-morrow. But progress towards this reality is being speeded up, and the way is being paved for it by an evolution of British authority.

Just as India is neither a colony nor a Dominion, so she is not, and cannot be, anything like a synthetic State guided towards independence in the same way as Iraq; nor, in connection with her, can anything be observed comparable with the inevitable transformation of British policy in the Persian Gulf. An absolutely distinct type of State is being slowly formed in the Indo-Gangetic plain and its geographical dependencies. It seems bound to be the product of collaboration, in accordance with rules still undetermined, between Great Britain and India. For British authority alone, supposing that it were strong enough to draft a plan and impose it, could accomplish nothing worth while; nor would the Indian populations, supposing they were left to themselves, succeed any better.

After all, what has to be taken into account is not merely what people want, but facts; and one essential fact, which nothing can blot out, is that the British have been in India for the past three hundred years. Whether what they have achieved there is approved or disapproved, there is no wiping out the past, for that is beyond the power of the will of men. The process of evolution must continue, hastened perhaps by some de Vriesian mutations; but these mutations themselves must inevitably be founded both on what has existed and what now exists.

What exists, among other things, is the fact that India is an imperial geographical centre in the British Empire. If that Empire were to be represented on a graph by a curve with several foci, India would appear as one of these foci, and perhaps the most important of them. At least, she would be second only to Great Britain herself.

Around the Indian Empire gravitates a whole world: a world which embraces the greater part of Islam, a dozen States, any number of colonies, and routes of communication which are among the most frequented in the world. Here live one-fifth of the human race. Here rules Britannia, who holds the trident of Poseidon. She rules over India, and she rules through India – but her rule is subject to evolution, just as all this very

varied world is subject to evolution. Here old agreements and treaties are in constant course of transformation. This transformation is leading the British thalassocracy into a new era. It might eliminate British
power altogether, but for the fact that this power
possesses a wonderful faculty of adaptation, which
constitutes its greatness and may assure its permanence.

VI

JAPAN: AN ISLAND EMPIRE WITH CONTINENTAL 'MARCHES'

THE ISLAND NATION AND THE MAINLAND

ALL the way from Kamchatka to Singapore, Asia is separated from the Pacific Ocean by coastal seas enclosed on the side of the ocean by an open-work barrier of islands, islets, and rocks.

From north to south, these coastal seas are as follows: the Sea of Okhotsk, enclosed from Kamchatka Point to Yezo by the Kurile Islands; the Sea of Japan, closely hemmed in, from Sakhalin to Korea, by the great islands of the Japanese archipelago; the East China Sea, separated from the Pacific Ocean by the double dotted line of the Riukiu Islands, and with one of its gulfs, the Yellow Sea, penetrating deeply in between Korea, Manchuria, and China; and the South China Sea, enclosed, far off shore, by the great islands of Formosa, the Philippines, Borneo, and Sumatra.

From the Kuriles to Formosa, all these islands are Japanese. It is true that the often ice-bound Sea of Okhotsk does not possess much importance, and that the South China Sea is so extensive, and several of its entrances are so wide, that it can scarcely feel any sense of encirclement. But the Sea of Japan is rightly so named. Now that, under the flag of the

Rising Sun, the southern part of Sakhalin has become Karafuto and Korea has become Chosen, all the 'live' coasts of this sea, both insular and mainland, are Japanese.

The Siberian Maritime Province has no coastal activity except at Vladivostok; and Vladivostok, despite its name, scarcely dominates the East from its situation at the end of a Japanese lake. The mainland shores of the East China Sea, on the other hand, are China at her most Chinese and her most densely populated. But the Yellow Sea is only half Chinese, and upon it Japan possesses to the north the great gate of autonomous Manchukuo and to the east the Korean coast. The belt of islands from Kiushiu to Formosa is wholly Japanese, profoundly, historically Japanese. The Riukiu – which Fernand Mendez Pinto wrote 'Lequio' – preserved through centuries of Chinese rule the Japanese traits of their population; and Kiushiu, the first land where the Europeans of the sixteenth century were amazed to discover Japanese civilisation, is probably the oldest possession of the Japanese people.

To the south-east, out in the Pacific Ocean, a great semicircle of islands, stretching from Shikoku to the Malay peninsula, sketches another and a more advanced maritime frontier, formed by the Bonin islands, the Marianas, the Carolines, Yap and the Pelews. All these islands have become Japanese: the first since sixty years ago, the rest by mandate as a sequel to the World War.

Thus, from desert Kamchatka to the politically uncertain Philippines, the island barrier which separates the Asiatic continent and its coastal seas from the Pacific Ocean and the American continent is entirely

Japanese. Here, over forty degrees of latitude, extends the domain of Japan: a domain both metropolitan and colonial, but a domain essentially insular and maritime, to which a mainland domain has only recently been added.

The value of this position is comparable with what the position of the British Isles would be if they were continued by a chain of islands stretching as far as the north of Norway and southwards as far as Morocco. Let us imagine, moreover, such an archipelago in course of the full development of modern civilisation, off shore from a mainland desolated by the economic and political chaos of the Middle Ages. We shall then have some idea how many, how varied, how unexpected may be the processes of interdependence, the problems of political geography, in such a zone of contacts.

The primary feature of this Japanese power, in chronological order as well as in the sphere of its present-day importance, is therefore its insularity: its geographical, ethnical, and political insularity. The great metropolitan islands were doubtless once islands of refuge, conquered lands, settlements of maritime races. The multiple elements in their population bear witness to this: the Ainos, who are attributed an Aryan origin, but who have almost ceased to count; the Mongol stock, which contributed old Chinese and Korean civilisation; the invaders come from the Malay peninsula or the Pacific, who gave the nation its refined type, its social organisation, its mythology, and its maritime vocation, which came to a standstill in the seventeenth century for the purpose of passive resistance to European intrigues; and also its surprising capacity for assimilation and adaptation, for absorbing foreign art and science and recreating them.

The Japanese race has become the very type of extremely dense insular population. An average of 347 inhabitants to the square mile is largely exceeded in Honshiu, and nearly reached in Shikoku and Kiushiu. In 1930 the metropolitan part of the Empire numbered 64,450,000 souls, and the colonial part about 27 million. This density of population impresses Europeans, and leads them to interpret Japan's foreign policy as a pursuit of colonies for her surplus people.

Nevertheless, we find that in Korea the Japanese number only 500,000 out of 21 million souls. Manchukuo is certainly a country of immigration; but this is, above all, Chinese immigration. During the past few years, 9 million peasants have fled from China, settled in Manchukuo, and proceeded to breed there. Among the new colonists are also 800,000 Koreans. But there are only 228,000 Japanese; and these, for the most part, are State officials, railwaymen, overseers, and workmen in industries, and merchants of every category. Similarly in Taiwan – the Japanese name for Formosa – 40 per cent of the Japanese are officials or employees, and only 2 per cent work on the land.

At the same time, it is unquestionable that, from its outset, the expansionist policy pursued by the Tokyo Government was inspired by the need for opening up territory to which its prolific people could emigrate. To-day this concern remains the basis of Japan's foreign policy; but it has become more complex.

Modern Japan is a great industrial and mercantile State whose superabundant population is more and more deserting the fields for the factories. Accordingly

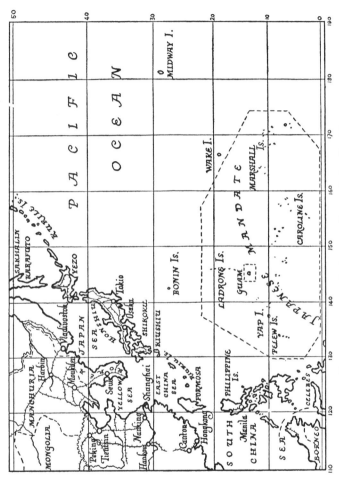

Japanese power in Mongolia and the Pacific

she has to export her manufactured goods and import food and raw material; make sure of foreign markets and colonial mines and fields; develop her external commerce, and organise colonisation for the purpose of exploitation, which, in her case, precedes colonisation for the purpose of peopling.

The direction of her expansion and her commerce are imposed upon Japan by her geographical situation. Placed off shore from Asia, looking out on an ocean dotted only by insignificant islets – Hawaii, the largest archipelago, more than three-quarters Japanese, shelters only 125,000 Nipponese, and is approaching its saturation-point – with States no less obliged to export their products on the other side of the ocean, metropolitan Japan depends economically on her colonies and on the mainland. She needs rice and – in proportion as the use of bread extends – wheat from Yezo, Korea, and Manchuria; soya beans from Manchuria; rice and sugar from Taiwan; fish from the cold waters of Yezo and Karafuto. The forests of the northern island supply timber for building, which is mostly in wood, and, together with bamboo from Formosa, paper-pulp. Karafuto and Taiwan possess oil and coal, but the coal-mines of Korea and Manchuria are much more important. Wherever there is any chance of success, cotton-growing is attempted.

Accordingly the countries which have been called 'overseas Japan' are suppliers of food and raw material, and they will be so more and more. Yezo and Karafuto, with their sparse population, may become to Japan what Beauce and Normandy are to France: an effect and a cause, at one and the same time, of a process of evolution in diet.

Now that the economy of the Empire of the Rising Sun is that of an industrial country, Japanese expansion is a function of export no less than import.   The markets for Japanese industry are on the mainland: the Korean market, the Manchurian market, and, over and above all, the Chinese market.   Now commerce requires internal security in the States concerned, and it requires international peace.   For this reason Japan, even if she were ready to remain indifferent, cannot put up with neighbours among whom economic disorder renders business relations precarious, while their political disorder spreads an atmosphere of unrest and insecurity throughout the Far East.

The interdependence which exists between the State holding the outer island barrier and the mainland compels Japan to interfere in the political life of China in order to defend her own economic life.   If we had on our maps colours indicating all the shades of politico-geographical relationships, we ought to tint China with a colour indicating a political interdependence, economic in its origin, between her and Japan.

Given a powerful State, with a genius for organisation and a strong will, if such an interdependence becomes established with a State falling into ruins, such as 'poor, sweet Korea,' annexation of a colonial character may follow.   If such an interdependence arises with a group of territories on the periphery of an anarchic State, which has more or less abandoned them, a process of economic organisation – beginning, for example, with a railway concession – may lead to political organisation and end in the creation of a new State: such is the history of Manchukuo.   Finally, if

the interdependence be between two great States, one
of which has fallen into chaos and civil war, we get
diplomatic and military intervention, such as that of
Japan in the Chinese Republic.

COLONISATION IN THE LAND OF MORNING CALM

Towards the end of the nineteenth century, Europeans were delighted to discover the charming romance
of the faithful 'Perfumed Spring.' So they waxed
sentimental when, in 1909, Japan annexed the 'Hermit
Kingdom' and set about modernising it. Distance lent
enchantment to 'sweet Korea,' just as the lapse of time
adorns far-off centuries, in which their modern
admirers might not find it so pleasant to live. Then,
very soon, people forgot all about Korea: even her
pretty Japanese name of Chosen, 'the Land of Morning
Calm.'

In the summer of 1931 she again came under the
spotlight. Brawls occurred in the north-east between
Chinese farmers and Korean rice-growers, and at the
same time anti-Chinese rioters made considerable disturbance at Ping-yang, the former capital, to-day a
city of 136,900 souls. An official protest from the
Chinese Government followed. Then, without even
wondering how it was that so many Chinese had settled
in a Japanese colony and come to play such a rôle
there, Europeans once more let oblivion cover their
dreams about these people clad in white and wearing
black top-hats.

Yet, amid all those tragic spots in political geography, where eager empires clash over the heads of
peoples who, though weary, are subject to sudden
awakenings of national spirit, what land could be more

moving than Korea, that 'march' of old China, that mainland 'march' of young Japan, that maritime 'march' of Siberia, where the Chino-Japanese War of 1894 and the Russo-Japanese War of 1904 were hatched ? Here twenty centuries have drawn around the Yellow Mediterranean an historical map as over-laden as that of the European Mediterranean.

Korea is a peninsula to the east of Asia, whose form and area recall peninsular Italy in 1914. A range of mountains follows the east coast. To the west, valleys, now well irrigated, descend to the China Sea. The climate is severe, with a temperature varying from 23° to 80°, although the latitude is that of the Greek lands between Crete and Bulgaria. Beyond the rivers Yalu and Tumen lies Manchuria. To the south, a strait, ten leagues wide, separates Korea from Tsushima and the nearest Japanese islands. Kiushiu and Honshiu are less than one hundred and thirty miles away. With these islands Korea has had economic and political relations since time immemorial.

Some two thousand years ago, Korea was divided into four kingdoms, and that of Mimana invoked Japan's aid against Siraki. The Japanese defeated the latter and put the former under tutelage. Since then, down to the twentieth century, the Korean States were more or less tributary to Japan. Commercial relations slackened onwards from the seventeenth century, when, on the Japanese side, trade was monopolised by the hereditary princes of Tsushima. But the age-old link persisted.

Among her ancestors Japan reckons old Korea, whose civilisation was the adornment of the Far East, where she alone adapted to her language a syllabic writing of

Aramean origin. The secret of the Satsuma pottery came to Japan from Korea, and so did the architects of the temples of Kyoto and Nagoya. Accordingly, when Japan put herself to school with the West in 1868, Korea felt entitled to accuse her of 'betraying' the culture of the East. On the other hand, in June 1909, on the eve of the Japanese annexation of Korea, the *Taiyo* described Japanese and Koreans as scions of the same race, who were destined to unite in one and the same nation. It added that, but for Japan, Korea, where political life was in complete decadence and all economic activity was rapidly dying, would be doomed to fall into the hands of a mainland empire, and that she therefore constituted a danger for the Japanese State. Accordingly it was both Japan's interest and her duty to control Korea.

An outpost of the Japanese archipelago on the mainland, Korea, as Professor Toru Terso put it thirty-five years ago, possessed the same importance in the Far East as did Constantinople in Europe. Meanwhile Russia, who had insinuated herself between the Ussuri and the sea from 1858 onwards, and reached the Korean frontier, proceeded to occupy Port Arthur, and was ready to link up medieval, crumbling Korea with the continent by a strong system of railways. No reaction was to be feared from China, who before long was to surrender plenty of other territory. On the other hand, any number of Japanese and Japanophiles, such as the French Professor Michel Revon, declared about 1894 – though nobody believed them at the time – that Japan would make war on China in order to save her from herself and modernise her, and, with her, the Far East as a whole.

The Trans-Siberian Railway, complemented by the Trans-Manchurian Railway, was linked with the Gulf of Pechili, and in 1903 the first express from Moscow reached Dalny (Dairen). At the same time, far from evacuating Manchuria, as she had undertaken to do, Russia sent General Bezobrazov forward to the Yalu. Korea was threatened, and with her Japan, who could foresee, in the near future, a Russian base on her own inland sea. Tokyo proposed an agreement with Russia to guarantee the independence of China and Korea ; but the slowness of the Tsar's diplomacy was matched by the swiftness of his military preparations. So came the Russo-Japanese War and the first of Russia's disasters.

So, too, came about the evolution of Korea. China's suzerainty over Korea had not been affirmed until about 1885; for before that time the Pekin Government had informed Europe and America that Korea had a free hand in her international relations. The Treaty of Shimonoseki, which put an end to the Japanese war with China in 1895, made Korea an independent State. The Treaty of Portsmouth, at the end of the war with Russia, placed Korea under a Japanese protectorate, which ended in annexation in 1910. Incapable of playing the rôle of a buffer State, Korea was bound to become either Russian or Japanese. It was Japan who carried her frontier forward to the Yalu.

Since then, Korea has become a prosperous country, energetically administered: all too energetically, according to the 'Young Koreans,' who, in the course of becoming modernised, have developed a spirit of independence. A short time ago, even some Japanese regretted that the moderate policy of Prince Ito had not been pursued. They were afraid lest going to the other extreme should reproduce those international dangers once represented by anarchic Korea.

But a process of adaptation has since taken place. In contact with realities, the theories of the Japanese administration have evolved like other theories, and the Japanese officials in Korea have caught the idea that, in colonial policy, assimilation is perhaps only another name for taking the line of least resistance. Moreover, Europeans and Americans, who have recently visited the old kingdom of Morning Calm, have come to the conclusion that Bolshevism is lacking in attraction for the Nationalists of Seul. At the same time, these observers are convinced that without Japanese framework Chosen would soon collapse. They hope to see her evolve towards political maturity, like Porto Rico and the Philippines.

The two contrasting pictures of Korea, one of the hermit kingdom, the other of the Japanese colony, make up a pretty diptych in human geography. On one side, we see the moribund State, in which commerce, industry, even agriculture have dwindled to nothing. No peasant dare keep a tree near his house; for, if he were not rich, he would have felled it for fuel; and, if he were rich, he could be squeezed. The result was that hay became the common fuel, and the result of that, again, was that, for lack of fodder, cattle disappeared. On the other panel of the diptych we see a country whose population has increased 50 per cent in twenty-five years. More than 1,900 miles of railway, and 12,000 miles of main and secondary roads, have been constructed. The capital, Seul (Keijo) numbers 350,000 inhabitants, Ping-Yang (Heijo) 136,900, Taikiu 101,000 – all of them cities with water, electricity, and public health services. The ports of Fusan (130,000 inhabitants), Chemulpo (63,600 inhabitants) and Gensan (40,000 inhabitants) possess up-to-date equipment. Schools have multiplied, industries have been established, the growing of rice and cotton has been developed, 1,600,000 cattle graze on the pastures, and millions of trees have been planted on the denuded hill-sides.

This Chosen, this new Korea, this Korea to some extent colonial, economically at once a purveyor to Japan and a customer of Japan, represents politically the modern form of a phenomenon of political geography which we wrongly tend to relegate to the past, but which, nevertheless, can easily be identified in various parts of the world of our time: the frontier zone, the buffer-State, the 'march.'

On a small-scale map, the almost uninterrupted line of the rivers Yalu and Tumen looks like the perfect type of a natural frontier. But the Japanese know very well that there is no such thing as a natural frontier, and that nothing is more artificial than a 'frontier line' – above all, perhaps, when it is marked by a river. Since they know very well, too, that in foreign policy, and notably in the matter of Asiatic expansion, Bolshevist Russia is the heiress and the continuator of Tsarist Russia, they have kept on organising their mainland frontier.

Chosen was their base on the Asiatic coast, bounded to the west by their first, fragile frontier-line, the Yalu-Tumen. Beyond it extended the so-called 'Eastern Provinces' of China: in fact, anarchical Manchuria.

Across this territory, ravaged by brigands, a year after the Treaty of Portsmouth, Japan installed the South Manchuria Railway Company, a regular chartered company. As its domain it had the railway running from the strong maritime base of Dairen to Changchun – to-day the capital of Manchukuo under the name of Hsinking – some seven hundred miles away to the north.

On either side of the line, the company controlled in theory ten yards of territory. All along the line it controlled factories, mines, settlements which were regular towns. Mukden itself was embraced in its sphere of action, and became the *de facto* capital of this strongly held railway-State; and 7,000 soldiers guarded the line. Such, for nearly a quarter of a century, was Japan's second 'western march.'

RAILWAY ZONES IN MANCHURIA

Manchuria, the fief from which sprang the last dynasty to reign over China, from 1644 to 1912, had been kept, by her imperial sons, isolated in the past, two centuries behind China herself. She was a land under a sleepy spell, where one emperor closed down a mine because its working might disturb the peace of his ancestors' spirits in their near-by imperial tomb. She was a forbidden land, barred by the primitive form of passport, the *lu-piao*, against colonisation by the hordes of Chinese who were always ready to overflow their frontiers.

On the other hand, by her geographical position Manchuria was doomed to become a sphere of feverish international activity. Since she surrounded the region which linked the peninsula of Korea with the mainland, she must inevitably be regarded by the Japanese Empire as a mainland 'march.' Nor could Russia fail to seek, by way of Manchuria, a route to the Yellow Sea, that gateway to ice-free waters, with its straits which she supposed she could easily make her own.

On this land of the past, two political and economic powers clashed in the most modern of pursuits. Their means of penetration were the railways, in the hands of companies with State backing. So the latent vocation implicit in the geographical entity of Manchuria became awakened. A natural force found itself freed and proceeded to develop.

Manchuria, with her slow winter cartage over frosty ground or frozen river, her caravans of draught and pack camels, became a land of railways. Since 1876, the whole of China has constructed only about 8,000 miles of railway. Manchuria, who laid her first rail a score of years later, soon had more than 4,000 miles. She commanded the termini of the transcontinental line from the Atlantic Ocean to the 'Mediterranean Sea' of the Pacific and the plexus of railway lines where the intermingled interests of two rival empires met. To this external action of the railways was added an internal action. Like those of the American Far West and the Canadian prairies, the great Manchurian lines created a zone of activity, tillage, and settlement, which became the backbone of a new State.

The entrance of Manchuria into modern diplomatic life dates from April 1895, when, at the instance of Russia, France, and Germany, Japan renounced taking advantage of the clause in the Treaty of Shimonoseki by which China ceded her the peninsula of Liaotung.

The next year, Russia signed a secret treaty with China which authorised her to construct a railway from west to east across Manchurian territory. This enabled Russia to avoid a long detour by way of the northern bend of the Amur river, and to take her trans-Siberian railway straight to Vladivostok through the provinces of the Amur and Kirin. Then, in 1898, she obtained a twenty-five years' lease of the Liaotung peninsula, with the right to link it by railway with the trans-Siberian. Henceforth the main lines of the Manchurian system were settled: one line running from west to east in the north, and, from Harbin, another line running from north to south, which led, by way of Mukden, to a port at the end of the Liaotung peninsula on a sea always free from ice.

In 1905, the Treaty of Portsmouth transferred from vanquished Russia to Japan the lease of the Liaotung peninsula – now the Japanese colony of Kwangtung – and the rights over the railway line from Changchun to Port Arthur. These transfers were recognised by China a little later. From this moment dates the separation of the Manchurian railways into two systems: in the north, the Chinese Eastern Railway – in fact, a Russian system – with the main line Manchuli–Tsitsihar (Angangchi)–Harbin–Vladivostok, and the branch line Harbin–Changchun; in the south, the South Manchuria Railway – in fact, a Japanese system – with the main line Changchun–Dairen, and branches towards Korea.

These Manchurian railway companies had all the appearance of great chartered companies endowed with almost regal rights. The northern company suffered from the European war and the Russian

Revolution; and in 1924 this company, the Chinese Eastern Railway, was further weakened by the Soviet Government's agreement to share administration of the system with China. For this reason, the railway resources of the country, and its centre of prosperity, developed in Southern Manchuria, around the Japanese South Manchuria Railway Company.

The basis of its organisation was the railway concession. From Changchun to Dairen and Port Arthur, the Japanese made the railway one of the rare double-track lines in the Far East, and they replaced the military railway from Mukden to Antung by a broad-gauge line. The terminus of the Kwangtung section of the railway was transferred from Port Arthur to Dairen, which became the second commercial port on the Chinese coast.

But the company not only developed the railway and the port. It not only created ancillary services such as posts and telegraphs on behalf of the State. It had also a territory of its own to administer. All along the railway line it received a strip of soil with a minimum width of eleven yards, which was increased to about nineteen yards at junctions. At certain parts of the main lines, this land for development might extend to four hundred and forty yards. At the stations, little tracts of territory were conceded to the company, and here arose villages and sometimes whole suburbs, as at Mukden, where the railway suburb is linked to the Chinese city by the commercial city. Finally, the company had an industrial domain consisting of coal-mines, iron-mines, and great stretches of forest.

Thus was constituted a kind of industrial State of odd shape, with a length of seven hundred miles – that of the railways themselves – and an area of about a hundred square miles. This State attained remarkable prosperity, and its public services were organised with an enlightened liberalism which many a political State might envy. For example, its health services yielded particularly striking results in a country where contagious diseases, notably plague, were rife in an endemic state.

But China found no satisfaction in all this, and she deliberately put obstacles in the way of the South Manchuria Railway, among other things by duplicating the Japanese lines with competing·lines, though she was bound by treaty not to construct any. For example, she endeavoured to divert the Changchun–Dairen traffic to Hulutao, a Chinese port which a Dutch company had developed on the Gulf of Pechili, close to the line from Mukden to Peking (now known as Peiping). With the same object, she constructed a line from Tahuchan to Tungliao which would link up with Taonan, and thus provide a direct line from Peiping to Tsitsihar and connect China with the trans-Siberian railway without using any Japanese line. Similarly a line was constructed from Mukden to Kirin by way of Heilung. On the other hand, the Japanese were not able to complete the section east of Tunhua of their lines from Changchun to Seichin, the Korean northern port, until the spring of 1933, thanks to their military action in the south. Meanwhile the Chinese did not put in hand the line from Changchun to Tailai which they had undertaken to construct with Japanese capital.

Manchuria, though officially Chinese, had nevertheless rapidly become a country of Russian influence in

The Continental 'Marches' of Japan

the north and Japanese influence in the south. Further,
any security in this country was assured only by the
troops who guarded the railways.   Some 50,000
brigands, most of them well mounted, former Chinese
soldiers – many of whom were Manchus – who were
ready to join up again whenever some 'war lord' should
gather an army, regularly raided the territory between
the mountains and forests of the Khingans and the
Shan Alins.   The railways themselves were not ex-
empt from their aggression, and in the course of recent
years the South Manchuria Railway reckoned an
average of one attack a day on one point or another
of its lines.   Nevertheless, on account of their guards –
Russian in the north, until 1924; Japanese in the south,
from 1905 onwards – the railways constituted zones of
security along which Chinese settled: either regular
colonists or seasonal agricultural labourers who had at
last managed to obtain free access to the 'Eastern
Provinces.'

We know neither the exact number nor the exact
ethnical composition of the Manchurian population.
According to some estimates, there are scarcely one
million Manchus left, and Chinese account for nine-
tenths of the population.   In fact, the 'native' element
cannot exceed 20 million, even if to Manchus and
Mongols we add Chinese settled in the country since
the sixteenth century.   Recent immigrants comprise
about 9 million Chinese peasants; 800,000 Korean
pioneers, whose lands the Chinese show themselves
eager to acquire as soon as the Koreans have turned
them into the best rice-fields in the world; and, finally,
less than 300,000 Japanese: merchants, clerks, and
workmen.   The Japanese, unlike the Chinese and the

Koreans, do not accommodate themselves to the hard life and the low wages of up-country Manchuria.

Meanwhile the economic life of Manchuria, transformed by the railway, has evolved rapidly. Agricultural production has doubled in fifteen years. The harvest of soya – that bean, serving all purposes, which is to the Manchu what the date is to the Bedouin – amounted in 1930 to 5,300,000 tons. Cereals – *kaoliang*, millet, wheat and rice – yield increasing crops. Textile and agricultural industries – especially flour-milling and oil-milling – have been established. Between 1907 and 1929, foreign trade increased from eight million pounds to over a hundred million pounds.

The world economic crisis led to a slight decrease in this figure in 1930; but this diminution was only temporary. Like a Nile due to the industry of men, amid the fields which it has made fertile and the colonies which it has attracted, the railway crosses what for so many centuries was poverty-stricken, almost desert Manchuria.

But such an economic transformation, in a geographical environment situated as Manchuria is, necessarily involved a profound political transformation. Manchuria has become what one may call in space, and perhaps also in time, an intervening State, now known as Manchukuo.

THE INTERVENING STATE OF MANCHUKUO

Manchuria has always been pre-eminently a frontier region. She lies beyond the Great Wall of China, outside the domain of the *Han*, those peaceful farmers and traders of the valleys and the great rivers. In ancient

times she separated China from the barbarians of the
north. During the centuries when China was subject
to Manchu emperors, these emperors made a point of
maintaining a frontier between their country of origin
and the empire which they had conquered. Like their
ancestors, they remained Manchus. Every five years,
with great pomp, they had their archives transported
to Mukden. Peking, in their eyes, was always a foreign
city.

Similarly, for the Chinese in general, Manchuria was
above all an intervening land: formerly, between their
State and the wastes where Mongol horsemen rode; in
modern times, between their State and the Western
world which the Russian railway brought to their doors
across Siberia. To stop the West on the threshold of
real China, the cession of Manchuria struck them as a
reasonable price, about which it was scarcely worth
their while to argue.

The Russian advance towards the ice-free sea demanded the crossing of Manchuria from west to east
by the railway running to Vladivostok and the Sea of
Japan, and from north to south by the branch leading
to the Yellow Sea. But a transcontinental railway of
such importance could not have its terminus in a
country where Chinese disorder prevailed – especially
Chinese disorder with a coefficient, so to speak; for
Manchuria was not China properly speaking, but
simply a kind of antechamber on the threshold of
China, without economic importance, with a declining population, with its cities falling into ruin, with its
fields abandoned to Mongol nomads and Tunguse
brigands.

Manchuria's exact status remained vague. Then,

in 1896, Li Hung Chang signed a secret treaty with Russia, by which he practically surrendered the territory of Manchuria to her. Manchuria was thus doomed to be the unhappy theatre of the imminent war, which the old Chinese Minister knew very well was coming. Her fate was worse than that merely of a frontier region. It was the fate of a kind of outer 'march,' condemned to change of master without any respect for its people.

For if, after this transaction, Russia had been victorious in 1904, Manchuria would automatically have become a Siberian province. Instead of being a Chinese 'march,' she would have been transformed into a Russian Far-Eastern 'march,' face to face with Korea, Japan's western 'march.' Between them would have run the Yalu-Tumen ditch: the very type of those so-called natural frontiers which one might believe Nature gives men in order to provide them with pretexts for war.

It was from the end of the Russo-Japanese War, from 1905 onwards, that Manchuria came to assume her contemporary appearance: the meeting-place of the forces, political, economic, and human, of Russia, Japan, and China. During all the period which followed, she did not really belong to anybody. Anybody could settle there, at his own risk and peril. Plenty of Chinese officials remained: but they were incapable of maintaining any kind of social or political order. The sole real authority was that of the brigands, who were soldiers on occasion, then turned back into brigands, and then became soldiers once more, in accordance with their leadership, the time of year and the height of the *kaoliang*.

With the native population sparse and declining, the mass of the people who occupied the country and brought it into cultivation came more and more to be a swarm of colonists, Chinese peasants from the south, fleeing before the pillaging soldiery of the rival 'war lords,' whom the Government recognised by Europe feared no less than the Bolshevist Kuomintang. They flocked by the million into Manchuria, where, to be sure, they were plundered from time to time by the brigands, but where there at least existed an organised, policed territory, in which they could labour with some hope of themselves reaping the soya they had sown. This territory was the railway zone, guarded by the Russians in the north and by the Japanese in the south. It was soon to become almost wholly Japanese.

For Manchuria was now to take the place of Korea as Japan's western 'march.' The Yalu-Tumen line was no longer her furthest frontier. The railway zone from Dairen to Harbin, with its branches and its hinterland – this was the true frontier between the organised world and chaos. In the 'Eastern Provinces' as a whole, a struggle went on between the Japanese penetration and organisation and the military anarchy of the 'war lords.' Their bands swept through Chinese territory, pillaging turn about the different provinces and cities which they took from one another or exchanged amicably among themselves. Meanwhile Europe received reports of more or less imaginary battles. Such a spectacle was witnessed as that of Chang-Tso-lin, and, after him, his son Chang-Hsueh-liang, Manchus themselves though they were, coming to an understanding with the Nanking Government and operating in the western provinces. So the Chinese colonists, who had no intention of being merely temporary immigrants, rapidly acquired – so far as the average Chinese is capable of interesting himself in public affairs – political views very like those of the natives.

Order, therefore, was introduced from outside. The railway made Japanese peace penetrate the 'Eastern Provinces': at the outset, in the zone of the South Manchuria Railway. Then, on both sides, the need was felt for extending this zone of peace and security. This need explains the foundation, on March 1, 1932, of a new State: Manchukuo. The frontier 'march' thus became, under the aegis of Japan, a distinct political entity.

Under the aegis of Japan: that is the point. Jurisconsults have long since unearthed and annotated texts, and employed them for arriving at varying views about Japan's rôle on this creation of Manchukuo. If we confine ourselves to the facts, Japan appears to be the one authority which was capable of exerting an organising influence in the midst of the Far Eastern anarchy. The Government of Manchukuo, like her population, is made up of Manchus, Mongols, and Chinese, and little by little they will fuse and form a new nation. But, for the time being, what best guarantees the life of the new State is the support of Japan.

That support will not fail Manchukuo; for, to quote the conclusions of the Japanese delegates to the League of Nations, in their 'observations' of February 21, 1933, 'recognition of Manchukuo and giving her support constitute the sole means which can lead to a satisfactory solution of the Manchurian question and to the maintenance of lasting peace in the (Far) East.' Japan's determination not to swerve from these conclusions was manifested on the following March 27, when she withdrew from the League of Nations rather than accept the non-recognition of Manchukuo as a Sovereign State. On March 1, 1934, Pu-Yi, who as a child had been the last Manchu Emperor of China, and for the past two years had been head of the Government at Hsinking, was crowned emperor of the country which gave birth to his dynasty.

So for Manchuria, that Chinese, Russian, and Japanese 'march,' was substituted an intervening State, created and maintained with the support of Japan. The frontier zones were carried further west and south: into the Mongolias and to the Great Wall.

FRONTIER ZONES IN MONGOLIAN TERRITORY

When the Japanese troops advanced towards the south-west in the winter of 1932–3, we were told that Chinese patriots had sworn to defend Jehol to the last gasp, 'even if Nanking itself were taken.' Nanking was not even threatened, and Jehol was scarcely defended at all. In China 'war lords' and patriots are not always one and the same. Whether word went forth or not, whether what was intended took place or not, the fact remains on record that, after a lapse of two thousand years, some Chinese still remember the colonisation of the Emperor Wu. So the importance of Jehol in the sequence of China's northern frontiers was now understood.

A borderland in between Manchuria, Mongolia, and China proper, Jehol has some features in common with each of them. The mountains which continue the Great Khingan southwards to the Lwan Ho bound it on the west; and from their peaks, which rise to nearly five thousand feet, the country descends to the valley of the Liao. Physically, therefore, Jehol constitutes the south-western part of Manchuria, and its great rivers belong to the Liao basin. Politically, however, it was a part of Inner Mongolia, until the recent date when the Chinese Government attached it to the three 'Eastern Provinces.'

On maps dating back a few years, Jehol is not always to be found. So it is not a distinct province. The south of its territory, as far as the Shara Muren, is merely the northern part of Chili, and therefore is in China proper, though it lies outside the Great Wall. Everything about it suggests a transit territory, and the 'Jehol gap' was always one of the routes of Manchu and Mongol invasion. The capital itself, in the extreme south of the district, is not much more than a hundred miles away from Peking, with which it is linked by a motor-service. Jehol used to be the favourite summer resort, the Versailles, of the Manchu emperors, a city of palaces, temples, and gardens, and also a city of refuge. The Etiquette Department of the Imperial Palace used to announce that the Emperor had 'gone to hunt at Jehol,' meaning that the Son of Heaven had had to flee from Peking because of civil commotion or foreign invasion.

The province made up of the Jehol district – detached from Chili – and of Mongol territory was included for administrative purposes in Inner Mongolia. This latter expression perhaps requires to be defined. Article III of the Provisional Constitution of the Chinese Republic, dated March 10, 1912, declares that 'the territory of the Republic comprises the twenty-two provinces, Inner and Outer Mongolia,

Tibet and Shanghai or Tsinghai (Kukunor).' But in the Provisional Constitution, dated June 1, 1931, only Outer Mongolia and Tibet are separately mentioned. Inner Mongolia is included with China properly speaking in the expression 'the different provinces.'

The provinces of Inner Mongolia are Jehol, Chahar and Suiyuan. Jehol is much the most important of the three, for it alone has four and a half million inhabitants: more than half the whole population of Inner Mongolia. At least in its southern region, this population is mostly made up of Chinese colonists. For that matter, in all Inner Mongolia there are barely one million four hundred thousand Mongols, or about one-sixth of the total population. It is especially in Jehol that the proportion of Chinese is high.

From the moment of her foundation, Manchukuo, as her Ministers informed the Lytton Commission in August 1932, regarded the Great Wall as her south-west boundary, and therefore considered Jehol as being part of her territory. China herself, in 1927, had linked the 'special district' of Jehol, created by the revolutionary Government, with the three 'Eastern Provinces.'

If one superimposes political and demographic maps on a physical map, one notices at once that the boundaries of Manchukuo and the Mongol territories – administratively or ethnically speaking – do not correspond with the facts of physical geography. The west part of the province of Heilungkiang is on the western slope of the Great Khingan, where the district of Barga – also called Hulunbuir, from the names of the two lakes, Hulun and Buir, which are its outstanding geographical features – is inhabited by Mongol tribes grouped in 'banner' federations. The same applies to the north-west of the province of Fengtien, where 'banners' form the powerful federation of Chelimu, a political and social organisation similar to those which occupy the greater part of Jehol: the Chaota federation in the north, and the Chosatu federation in the south.

Mongol territory, therefore, extends widely over the eastern slope of the mountainous folds which bound the Liao basin to the west. One may put it that the province of Jehol, placed by administrative order in Inner Mongolia, was placed by Nature in Manchuria; while the district of Barga, though part of a Manchurian province, belongs physically to Mongolia.

These Mongols, unlike the Manchus, who have all but disappeared, have preserved their strongly marked characteristics as proud, indomitable nomads. They resent being driven towards the desert in proportion to the advance of the Chinese colonists, who, by their patient, ant-like labours, pioneer the country and settle their swarming families in it. If these colonists scarcely remember Wu, the Mongols have never forgotten Genghis Khan and the raids of their ancestors, who penetrated deeply in the land of the *Han*, those farmers and merchants, and made them pay plentiful tribute. Accordingly the Jehol federations, the Chaota and the Chosatu, keep in permanent contact with the Fengtien 'banners,' and they long since organised 'committees' ready to fight for independence. So, just as Jehol is geographically in Manchuria, it also possessed an ethnical element which hailed the creation of Manchukuo with the utmost satisfaction.

This   fact   explains   the   first   sentence   in   the communication made by Mr. Hsieh Chieh Shih, Minister for Foreign Affairs of Manchukuo, to his colleagues abroad: 'I have the honour of informing you that the Provinces of Fengtien, Kirin, Heilungkiang and Jehol, the Tungsheng Special District,[1] *and Mongolian Mengs (Leagues) under several Banners*, have united themselves to establish an independent Government, severing their relations with the Republic of China, and created "Manchukuo," the State of Manchuria, on March 1, 1932.'

Jehol is therefore the meeting-point of the Mongol, Chinese, and Manchu worlds (I use the word 'Manchu' in its present-day sense, not its historical or ethnical sense); and it was a singularly striking spectacle to see Japanese and Chinese troops meet at the Versailles of the Manchu emperors, whose last scion was presiding at Hsinking, under the aegis of Japan, over a State peopled by a handful of survivors of his race, amid Chinese peasants and with Mongol horsemen hovering on the horizon.

But it is not solely in the south-west of Manchukuo that the Mongols have reappeared in history after an eclipse lasting several centuries.[2] The first statements officially published by the new State recalled the question raised not only by Inner Mongolia, but also by Outer Mongolia.

Outer Mongolia, though it was named in the Chinese Constitution among the component parts of the

[1] The former railway zone.

[2] The Mongols are now estimated to number some five million souls; two million in Manchukuo; one million in Inner Mongolia; one million in Outer Mongolia; and perhaps one million divided among Chinese Sinkiang, the Tibetan province of the Kukunor, and the Soviet republic of the Buriats in Siberia.

Chinese Republic, is in fact an 'independent' State which has joined the Soviet Union: in other words, a Russian vassal State forbidden to foreigners and their trade – and among such 'foreigners' figure the Chinese. On the other hand, Japanese diplomatic documents, when referring to the north-east marches of China, always use the expression: 'Manchuria and Mongolia.' Any map which included Mongolia in the political territory of China would be as misleading as one which placed Korea and Manchukuo in it. Russia and Japan between them have pushed the territory of China to the south of the Great Wall, and reduced it to China properly so-called, and, for the moment at least, Tibet.

Now that two new States, Manchukuo and Outer Mongolia, have appeared on the map bordering China, the real frontier zones must be regarded as lying further to the west in Mongol territory. Beyond the Great Khingan and Jehol, the limit between Manchukuo and the two Mongolias is marked neither by any physical feature, nor by any difference between the populations in origin or political organisation. The Russians have sold the Chinese Eastern Railway to Japan, and they no longer take any interest in the north of Manchukuo, diverting their attention to Chinese Turkestan; while the Japanese are keeping an eye on Dolon Nor, at the entrance to the province of Chahar. The Chinese, driven back beyond the Great Wall, continue to work out their obscure destiny in their proper country of the Hwang Ho and the Yang-tze-kiang. The region to the north of the Hwang Ho thus becomes, so to speak, a new 'march.' In 1935, when the Japanese legation at Nanking was elevated into an embassy, the Nanking Government gave Japan an undertaking that any military activity and any national-ist organisation in this region should be suppressed. Mainland Japan is slowly but surely rounding off her domain.

OLD DIVISIONS AND NEW STATES

Observation and analysis of the natural elements affecting China, Russia, and Japan, which constitute the basis of the 'problems' and 'questions' of the Far East, reveal systems in evolution: processes of inter-dependence in course of organisation; frontier zones in course of movement; 'marches' in course of creation.

The passive human element is represented by the native populations, Korean, Manchu, Mongol, and Chinese, whose organisation is crumbling, and who are scarcely capable of more than reflex action in the economic and political sphere – though it is not impossible that a revival of Mongol nationalism may take place under the influence of the Prince of the Western Sunit, Te Wang, whom both the Chinese and the Russians find it expedient to conciliate so long as peace prevails in Eastern Asia. The active human element, capable of recognising the gifts of Nature, turning them to account, and making plans for develop-ing them, and at the same time determined and able to carry out such plans, once seemed to be supplied by Europe, and especially by Russia. But it is in fact around the nucleus of Japan that the immense synthesis of Far Eastern political geography is being worked out. In the Japanese islands off shore from the mainland the process of contact, the process of evolution, of the peoples and the civilisations of Eastern Asia, mainland

and insular, have produced the political human type which has succeeded in merging in one and the same nation the intellectual and material resources of East and West.

The essential part, the metropolitan part, so to speak, of the Japanese State took shape in the great islands of its archipelago. Constant communication linked these islands with the mainland, and with the strings of islets from Kamchatka to the Malay peninsula. The population of historic Japan came from the tropical islands and from the mainland – and probably the prehistoric population which we call native came from the mainland too. Economic and intellectual interdependence became established by way of Kiushiu and Korea. To the west, therefore, Japan's first frontier – in other words, her first point of contact with the mainland – was the sea; and her first frontier zones were the inland seas that wash the mainland. At different periods – some of them quite remote – this frontier expanded into a peninsular 'march': Korea, where Japan long ago had commercial and political interests, and even played the rôle of suzerain.

Korea's geographical situation marked her out to be the first mainland 'march' of contemporary Japan: a 'march' of the type created in the nineteenth century, which we may call the railway 'march.' Japan constructed a Korean railway system whose stations were centres of colonisation, though from the standpoint of developing the country rather than peopling it. Russia, by her railways from west to east and from north to south, similarly materialised her Manchurian frontier.

For a real frontier is not necessarily the line on either

side of which two opposing Powers stand face to face. The Yalu-Tumen line, despite the appearance of a 'natural frontier' which it doubtless displays on the map, in fact scarcely counted. The real frontiers of the empires which met in the Far East, the points of departure of their coming search for space, the strong centres of resistance which buttressed their acquisitions up to date, were the railway zones, destined to become the backbones of new political entities. They took shape first, and they would disintegrate last, just as the vertebral column exists from the embryo to the final destruction of the human skeleton.

As a peninsula, Korea was at once a maritime 'march' and a mainland 'march': the first stage along the road by which the Japanese nation, partly composed of continental elements, returned to the mainland after fashioning out of these elements, in its island crucible, a new body with a strongly marked personality.   As a part of the mainland, Manchuria was for Russia an inland 'march': the starting-point and the buttress of her quest for a maritime frontier, of her movement to enclose Korea, cut it off from the continent, and turn it into an island, while Vladivostok and the Liaotung peninsula supplied her with her first Far Eastern ports, with Chemulpo and Fusan to follow.   But vanquished Russia was not to become a maritime State on the inner seas of the Pacific; whereas Japan was to become a mainland State in Asia.

For Korea soon came to be something more than a 'march.' In her Japan found a territory which complemented her own insular economy and demography, such as she also sought in Yezo, Formosa, and Sakhalin.

For a time the two continental States, Japan and

Russia, were to come into contact in the former Russo-Chinese 'march': Manchuria, now in between Russian Siberia, the Kwangtung peninsula, and Japanese Chosen. Until March 1935, its frontiers were the zones of the South Manchuria Railway, that Japanese chartered company, and the Chinese Eastern Railway, that buttress of the Russian State.

But from time immemorial Manchuria had been the 'march' between China and the Mongol territories, and the old sovereignty of China over Manchuria – better described as the sovereignty of the Manchus over China – though it had become a fiction, supplied at least a conventional basis for Manchurian neutrality, pending the organisation of a Russo-Japanese 'march.'

Such was the setting of one of those modern conflicts in which historical title-deeds that have ceased to correspond with any reality are doomed to be over-ridden by energetic action in a spirit of realism. At a distance, this conflict may convey the impression of a clash between right and force; and equally unpleasant were the procedure which followed it and the interpretation of texts in which both parties indulged. But, if we look more closely, if we inform ourselves more exactly, we realise that dead things were disappearing into the dark, while living elements were rising into the light, continuing the uninterrupted cycle of evolution and renascence.

We see, too, what an advance these ideas mark over those of the old diplomatic school, when European nations, with the addition first of the United States of America and then of Japan, thought it quite permissible to carve up continents on a table covered with green baize. In the case of Africa, they cut away as they chose, taking care only not to offend the susceptibilities of their co-partners. In the case of China, they had in addition to take account of the empire which was being partitioned. So they invented the system of leased territories, which seemed to be a modernised form of the old trading settlements of a less distant East; but they failed to distinguish between abandoned 'annexes' of China and her impregnable nucleus.

Japan obtained the Kwangtung peninsula. Since this territory was not in real China, the process of evolution was able to continue, and Manchuria gradually adapted herself to the rôle – pending the regular status – of a mainland territory complementary to the island empire. The next phase was the creation of Manchukuo, born of the natural interdependence between the mainland and the Japanese islands.

It is a considerable distance from the leasing of Liaotung to the creation of Manchukuo. The two events are manifestations of two methods, of two conceptions of international relations, which are quite different. They mark a change, if not of era, at least of period: a transition from the old diplomacy, which was ready to approve anything that seemed to respect the letter of the law, even the 'renting' of territories, together with their inhabitants, to the new kind of action which troubles less about the form of procedure than about the matter of the lawsuit.

The creation of Manchukuo bears witness that the Powers no longer consider that putting the terms of a juridical contract on paper is enough to enable them afterwards to plead 'unquestionable rights.' They realise that their contracts will not be applicable and

lasting unless they take account of the peoples concerned and of the consent of those peoples. The stage
between territory-jobbing and the creation of a
national State is no short one. That stage has now
been covered in Asia.

It may be objected that Manchukuo is a State only
for window-dressing purposes, with a 'puppet Government.' Such is the charge made by those among the
Chinese who are incensed to find their once great
empire reduced to its national territory. They do not
stop to think that China could not avoid the fate of
similar empires, such as the Turkish and the Austrian.
They do not stop to think that, by virtue of its area
and population, China proper will still be a very great
State; and that she probably cannot be a very great
State until she is thus restricted to her own domain.

Even if, as these Chinese say, there is nothing at
Hsinking but puppets whose strings are pulled by
Japan; even if Manchukuo is nothing but a piece of
window-dressing, the fact nevertheless remains that
the Tokyo Government, when it might simply have
conquered and annexed Manchuria, decided instead
to create a national State and labour to bring a nation
to life again. If Japan did so because she thought it
right, that is a credit to her. If she did so because she
thought it expedient, that is a credit to our period.
In either case, brief is the night which separates the
twilight of old treaties from the dawn of new nations.

Russia, for her part, has created the Soviet republic
of Mongolia – Outer Mongolia. Japanese documents
say 'Manchuria-Mongolia' when they refer to the mainland territories concerned in Japan's recent political
action; but here we must understand that Inner

Mongolia is meant. Outer Mongolia has not yet much life of her own, and Russia does not take the same kind of interest in her as she used to take in Manchuria. Outer Mongolia is no more than a frontier 'march.' On March 23, 1935, the Soviet Government signed an agreement with Japan – who made herself responsible for the stipulated payments – by which Russia ceded to Manchukuo the Chinese Eastern Railway, which became the North Manchuria Railway. Two months later, the Soviet publicist, M. Karl Radek, interpreted this cession as the starting-point of friendly relations between the two countries, and he added : 'The Russian people, with their sense of realism, would never approve intervention by the Soviet Union in favour of revolutionary China. Soviet public opinion is unanimous in feeling that the fate of the Asiatic peoples, and especially of the Chinese people, depends on themselves.'

Such an attitude of detachment, expressed by the former rector of the Sun-Yat-Sen University, who once wanted to establish the Soviet revolution in China, but who now shares M. Stalin's views about non-intervention, demonstrates that, at least for the time being, Russia is abandoning her thrust towards the Yellow Sea, if not the Sea of Japan. If the Soviet Government is making this sacrifice in order to have a free hand in Chinese Turkestan, the two Mongolias will be the Russo-Japanese 'march' of to-morrow, the 'march' between the mainland State in the centre and north of Asia and the maritime State in the east of Asia.

Japan's domain, therefore, now extends between the Mongol 'marches' – and perhaps the Chinese 'marches' covering the region between the Great Wall and the Hwang Ho– and the oceanic 'marches' of the mandated islands in the neighbourhood of 170 degrees east longitude. The great islands of the archipelago of Nippon are the heart of the Japanese empire; the string of islands from Kamchatka to Formosa are its insular domain; Korea and Manchuria-Mongolia are its complementary territory on the mainland; and China is its customer and its principal provider.

It is singularly childish to 'denounce' all this as 'imperialism' and to oppose old juridical texts to these manifestations of life. A whole Japanese world is in course of organisation, based upon natural interdependence, and with a wonderfully complete range of political and economic relations among its parts. Politico-geographical analysis shows us how solid are its foundations: position, conditions of interdependence, demographic and economic elements; and such analysis tells us that we are witnessing the development in the Far East of a natural organism which is evolving normally towards stable equilibrium.

VII

THE UNITED STATES OVERSEAS

AMERICAN EXPANSION

ABOUT the New World Europeans entertain an idea no less simplified, and therefore no less confused, than most Americans' conception of the Old World. Ever since the end of the nineteenth century, Europeans, as they witnessed the activities of United States delegates at Pacific and Pan-American conferences, have not hesitated to denounce what they call 'American imperialism,' which, in their eyes, aims at domination of the Pacific Ocean and tropical America.

This view partly derives from a fairly widespread tendency to regard a sea-coast as a 'natural frontier.' A frontier, according to contemporary ideas, is in fact represented by a line. A sea-coast, a water-course, and even – at least on a small-scale map – a 'mountain-chain,' look like lines drawn by Nature. For this reason, people proceed to call them 'natural frontiers'; and, if they are at all inclined to mysticism, they consider such lines as landmarks provided by Providence in order to set limits to the development of States.

The 'fathers' of the United States appear to have reasoned precisely in this way. When Monroe put Alaska out of bounds for European colonisation in 1822 he did not claim it for the American Republic: he confined himself to limiting the action of the United States to the Western Continent. To be sure, the intervening provisional republic of Texas was annexed in 1845, and that of California in 1848; but these were metropolitan territories. On the other hand, the United States waited until 1867 to buy Alaska from Russia, until 1884 to organise it, and until 1912 to proclaim it a territory. After the War of Secession, the Senate – for reasons which were partly political – refused to acquire the West Indies. The Hawaiian Islands were not annexed until 1909.

It is not to be denied that, despite the bold enterprises of private individuals overseas, a traditional trend of thought stood in the way of committing the United States outside their 'natural frontiers': the St. Lawrence and the Great Lakes, the Gulf of Mexico, the Rio Grande del Norte, and the Pacific coast.

Nevertheless, anybody who looks for 'natural frontiers' on American soil at once discovers that, though the political map may be divided by frontiers drawn from east to west, the physical map showed a series of natural regions, between the Pacific and the Atlantic, whose axis lies more or less from north to south and cuts the frontiers of Canada and Mexico at right angles.

In fact, if you rid yourself of the idea of frontiers fixed by Nature, towards which States may reach, but beyond which they may not pass; if you take into account that real geographical factor, territory, whose frontier at a given period is only a conventional limit, then you find that the American State progressed from period to period, from region to region. It expanded from the Atlantic coast to the Alleghanies, and then to the valley of the Mississippi. It stopped first at the

Prairie, where the 'Indian frontier' was organised, and next at the Rockies. Then it went its way to the north-west and the great Oregon in the first half of the nineteenth century. At that time, some people saw a 'natural frontier' in the watershed between the Pacific slope and the Gulf of Mexico slope.

California, when Frémont set out to conquer it, was an island in between the mountains and the sea, which could be reached overland only by well-organised expeditions. This island was linked to American terri-tory only when the railway crossed the desert, like a bridge linking an island to the mainland. Going to California overland meant setting out on a dangerous adventure, while travelling to Hawaii was a common-place. The journey to California proved just as easy when it became a sea-voyage divided into two stages. To make this journey, gold-seekers crossed the isthmus of Nicaragua. The isthmus lands, therefore, formed part of an 'interior' high road of the United States.

Just as the Spaniards, as early as the sixteenth cen-tury, set off for the Far East by way of the west coast of America, so the Americans were simply following a tradition hundreds of years old when they set off for Hawaii and the Philippines. In other words, a sea-coast is not a frontier-line, but a passage-way between the mainland domain of a State and its maritime domain. The Pacific Ocean, in fact, is simply a 'march', strewn with islands, between the Whites and the Asiatics: an immense oceanic extension of the opposing empires of the Far West and the Far East.

In the Caribbean Sea, similarly, the United States have developed an insular tropical domain which simply continues the sub-tropical territory of the Old

South. There is no more break of continuity between
Florida and Porto Rico than there is between Pennsyl-
vania and Florida. The physical interdependence
between temperate territory and tropical territory has,
indeed, created economic links so natural and so strong
that Canada herself stretches out towards the West
Indies, for the purpose of exchanging her manufactured
products against the products of the orchards and
fields of the tropics.

The character of American economic and political
expansion outside the territory of the United States is
therefore very different from an imperialist enterprise
conceived and contrived by the will of a few men. It
is a continuation of the movement which formed the
metropolitan territory of the Republic; brought about
the first European navigation on the American coast
of the Pacific, and then to distant islands and as far as
Japan and the Chinese coast; and led the men of the
temperate regions to the tropical islands.

Doubtless on the branches of this tree, with its old,
deep roots, have been grafted new political ambitions
and economic intrigues; but we should not isolate them
from what is, so to speak, their natural support.
Otherwise we cannot recognise their true character,
estimate them at their proper value, and sum up their
real causes and the real scope of the diplomatic acts
which have resulted from them, and the order or
disorder which will result from them.

THE DISCOVERY OF CALIFORNIA AND THE PACIFIC
QUESTION IN THE SIXTEENTH CENTURY

The West Coast is the part of America least known
to Europeans, who are too ready to believe that they

have discovered the New World once they have acquired a vague idea of New York and Chicago. This American coast of the Pacific, however, possesses a very strongly marked personality of its own, and one attractive above all others from idyllic California to sylvan Washington. Its ports of San Francisco and Seattle are in every way comparable with the Atlantic emporiums. They are the 'golden gates' through which the Far West opens on to the Far East.

What country rich in legendary memories could attract us more than California ? Cortés and Díaz found a name for it in Montalvo's romance of chivalry, *Las Sergas del muy esforzado caballero Esplandián* – a poor sequel to *Amadis*, which Cervantes judged 'the best of all books of its kind.' The fabulous island of Queen Califia was called California, after the name of its sovereign. Above all, how can any Frenchman forget that the real founder of the State of California, in 1846, was General Frémont, son of a French colonist in Georgia ? American geographers, however, can claim him as their own, since he was an officer in the topographical service of the United States.

When Frémont set off with sixty-one men to conquer the land beyond the Rockies which was more or less governed by Mexico, he was reverting to the tradition of the great Spanish explorers of the sixteenth century. In November 1931 it was four hundred years since Cortés bought the ships which set off from Acapulco in the following May on a voyage of discovery along the coast to the north of Mexico. In this present second third of the twentieth century, we shall be able almost every year to celebrate the fourth centenary of some discovery in these regions.

They were discoveries made by seekers for gold, whose character, apart from their indomitable energy, had nothing very attractive about it.   One cannot but be surprised to find these great *conquistadores* obsessed by legends such as those of the 'seven cities' or the 'island of women,' and putting a childlike faith in the most preposterous stories of fabulous treasure. No sooner did some Indian or adventurer, contradicting himself a score of times, tell them about coasts where pearls abounded, cities where gold and silver were used for the commonest purposes, temples with their walls incrusted with precious stones, than they fitted out an expedition on the spot.

Those who travelled by sea found little but rocky, forbidding coasts, with land beyond them which could be made fertile only in the hands of modern scientific farmers.   Those who travelled overland, towards the east, crossed mountains and prairies where poverty-stricken Indians roamed.   At the best, they discovered in the interior only villages inhabited by people wearing cotton and buffalo-skins, who were usually hostile. Many an adventurer never came back.

Still, little by little the country became known. About 1540 Coronado penetrated probably as far as what is now Kansas.   Ships, following the coast, discovered the peninsula of Lower California, which was first taken for an island.   Ulloa, the first man to leave us a record of such a voyage, apparently reached, in 1540, the neighbourhood of the present frontier between the United States and Mexico.   As early as 1542, Cabrillo discovered Monterey Bay and perhaps ventured as far as the 41st degree of north latitude, a hundred leagues north of the bay on which San Francisco now stands.

The voyages of the second half of the sixteenth century had a wider scope than these coastal expeditions in search of Eldorados. Less than thirty years after Magellan's death, the crossing of the Pacific, the route to eastern Asia by way of the west, was constantly in everybody's mind; and other mariners set off in search of the 'North-West Passage.'

At the same time, we must not be too imaginative about the object of these voyages. It was a period of quarrels between the Portuguese and the Spaniards over the question of the ownership of the Moluccas, those islands rich in spices. The line of demarcation between the domains of the respective sovereigns, drawn by the Pope in 1493, and rectified the following year by the Tordesillas agreement, was very difficult to recognise in the sphere of fact. Were the Moluccas and the Philippines in the domain of Spain or in that of Portugal? It was in this form that the Pacific 'question' presented itself four hundred years ago. In 1529 the Moluccas were declared Portuguese. There remained the Philippines.

To settle this Pacific question, the American coast was taken as a base. It was from this coast that Spain, then the great American Power, set off to take possession of the Tagal archipelago. In 1550, when Urdaneta fitted out a trans-Pacific expedition in New Spain, he was already familiar with the route by way of the Ladrone Islands, now known as the Marianas, which was favourable at the beginning of the autumn, and the route by way of the south-west to New Guinea, which it was necessary to take 'from November 10 to

January 20.' He seems to have chosen a spring route. This route of his followed the west coast of America northwards, in Cabrillo's wake, to the neighbourhood of the bay of San Francisco. Thence, after reconnoitring the coast beyond Cabrillo's explorations, a course was set for the west, 'to discover what lies between this country and the Philippines.' Urdaneta, Arellano, Aguerra, and de Legaspi crossed the Pacific and returned to Acapulco. They brought back with them information which placed the Philippines in the States of the King of Spain.

Exploration of the American coast drew attention to the question of a 'North West Passage,' whose entrance in the Atlantic the English were now seeking. Recalling the theory (perhaps based on a sentence of doubtful authenticity in Marco Polo) that a strait, the Anian Strait, existed between America and Asia – in the neighbourhood where the Behring Strait was to be discovered in the seventeenth and eighteenth centuries – some Spanish mariners conceived the idea of sailing up the west coast of America to this strait, rounding the new continent eastwards, and so reaching Europe. But they do not appear to have received much encouragement from the Spanish authorities, who had no interest in making known yet another route towards the wealth of New Spain. So simply coastal exploration was continued; and from one of the more interesting of these voyages, that of Vizcaino, resulted the plan for a colony at Monterey.

Accordingly, at the beginning of the seventeenth century – Vizcaino's voyage was in 1602 – no progress had been made beyond the coast of present-day California; and there had been no penetration into the interior, where the gold-mines remained unknown for two and a half centuries. It was not until the last quarter of the eighteenth century that the north-west coast, to-day Canadian, was visited by Spaniards, by Cook, and by La Pérouse. From this period, too, date those missions in California whose ruins are one of the objects of historical pilgrimage popular with American tourists. The sixteenth-century expeditions left little or no trace except narratives and maps.[1]

PACIFIC NAVIGATION AND THE ANNEXATION OF THE HAWAIIAN ISLANDS

When Secretary of State Stimson, speaking about American policy in the Philippines at the end of 1931, said that the United States were *now* a Great Power in the Pacific Ocean and on its Asiatic side, he was displaying an exaggerated modesty.

It was so long ago as 1784 that a ship flying the Stars and Stripes first entered the port of Canton. Fifteen American ships arrived there in 1787, and only English ships were more numerous. As the Pacific coast was not yet part of the United States, these American ships, starting from New England, had made the voyage by way of the long and difficult route through the Strait of Magellan. Cook sighted Hawaii in 1778. So early as 1792, Vancouver found Americans there. In 1824, twenty-four American whalers were to be found at Honolulu at one and the same time; and in 1846, out of the four hundred and ninety-five whalers which

---

[1] In 1931 the California Historical Society published a book, due to the erudition of Mr. Henry R. Wagner, *Spanish Voyages to the North West coast of America in the Sixteenth Century*, which contained some very fine reproductions of contemporary documents and old maps.

dropped anchor in this port, three-quarters were American.

In 1842, moreover, even before Oregon and California were in the Union, the President of the United States declared that the Republic would not allow any nation to take possession of the Hawaiian archipelago. Finally it was an American, Commodore Perry, who, in 1854, reopened foreign trade with Japan, whom Jesuit intrigues had disquieted to such a point that ever since the sixteenth century she had shut herself up even more hermetically than China herself.

The War of Secession and the fatigue which followed it made the United States neglect their Navy, which was obsolete just at the moment when it would have been particularly valuable. They forgot all about Hawaii, the Pacific, and the East. Nevertheless, in 1874 American marines were sent to suppress disorder in the Hawaiian archipelago, and in 1876 the Republic signed a treaty of reciprocity with the island kingdom. But there was as yet no annexation, nor was there after American intervention in 1889. The Americans, in 1893, merely replaced the reigning dynasty by a republic. Then the history of Texas repeated itself, and in 1909 Hawaii became American, two years after the Philippines.

Such are the two bases of American operations in the Pacific. They are as unlike in every way as they could possibly be.

About midway between the Californian coast and Japan, the Hawaiian archipelago constitutes an almost unavoidable port of call of all crossings of the Pacific in the northern hemisphere; and it is the junction of the routes between Australia, America, and Asia. The cutting of the Panama Canal endowed it with new life.

These volcanic islands, with a fertile soil and a very mild climate – even though the sun shines there less constantly than tourist-agent booklets would have us believe, and the rainy season sometimes lasts for months – are covered with a sub-tropical vegetation whose brilliance and luxuriance defy imagination. They used to be one of the happiest lands in the world, peopled by a very fine race. But the primitive charm of the islands is dead, and the native race is rapidly disappearing. It is the penalty it has to pay for its matchless situation on the oceanic main routes.

A century ago, there were still one hundred and thirty thousand Hawaiians. In 1872, there were barely fifty-seven thousand. To-day only a score of thousands remain, together with as many half-breeds whose native blood is mixed with Chinese, Japanese, and sometimes Portuguese. The aboriginal population survives in its purity only in the less frequented islands. The ukulele-players who welcome winter visitors, the sellers of wreaths of flowers, and the *hula-hula*-dancers in their fibre or *tapa* skirts are now nothing more than professionals hired and costumed by the organisers of world-tours to provide 'local colour.'

While the gradual disappearance of a native race is a thing only too commonplace in 'ocean paradises,' a demographic phenomenon more peculiar to Hawaii is the creation of a new people, and perhaps – in the more or less near future – a new race. At the same time as the Hawaiians are dying out, the population of the archipelago is increasing. It grew from one hundred and fifty-four thousand souls in 1900 to three

hundred and sixty-eight thousand in 1930: an increase
of 139 per cent in thirty years. It is still a mixture, not a
combination. Asia is represented by one hundred and
twenty-five thousand Japanese and twenty-five thousand Chinese. Forty thousand Filipinos have settled in
the islands. The thirty-four thousand Americans must
not mislead us: nearly half of them are soldiers and
sailors. Finally, a certain number of Porto-Ricans
have come from the West Indies, and from Europe
some twenty-seven thousand Portuguese, who, almost
alone among Europeans, are able to work with impunity in tropical lands. Their immunity, according
to some authorities, is due to very old-established
African infiltration into certain parts of Portugal.

Cross-breeding is common among all the races, with
the exception of the Americans, who officially steer
clear of coloured people. But unhappy contacts sometimes occur. Hawaii was 'big news' in the United
States Press in 1932 on account of a somewhat scan-
dalous trial which recalled the tradition of negro-
lynchings in the Southern States, and led to an American officer being found guilty of the murder of a native.
Admiral Pratt, testifying in this connection before a
Senate commission, said that sexual offences were
serious and frequent in the islands, where any other
form of crime is rare, owing to the fact that 'women
tourists are too friendly to the natives. This creates a
difficult situation for the white women in the Navy
colony, because the natives do not discriminate.'

The dregs of Honolulu inevitably propagate the vices
of all races. As for Polynesian charm, here is what a
resident in the Hawaiis, Miss V. Dominus, recently
said in an interview published in the *Montreal Gazette*:

'There are very few palms to give mythical shelter to the youths who are supposed to sit beneath them strumming sweet music for the maidens. Of course there can be seen *hula-hula* dances, put on by the tourist bureau for the delectation of the visitor; but it is not the real Hawaii. Much publicity has been given to the famous beach of Waikiki on Oahu Island; but it is more like Coney Island than anything else.'

But, if the old-time islands are 'dead as earth,' a new Hawaii has arisen. Honolulu is a great American business city, complete with office-buildings and tramways, inhabited by one-third of the population of the archipelago. Rice-growing, *taro*-growing and cattle-breeding are surpassed in importance by fields of coffee and groves of banana-trees, orange-trees, and pear-trees; and the world's largest factory for canning pineapples is just outside Honolulu. More than anything else, however, sugar-cane, cultivated by processes which give the highest possible yield, is the great source of agricultural wealth. So far as this product is concerned, Hawaii is surpassed only by Cuba, India, Java, and Brazil. Americans settled in Hawaii have no desire to see Philippine sugar freely enter the United States indefinitely.

On the other hand, Hawaii gives the metropolis something to worry about from the demographic point of view. Any person born in Hawaiian territory is an American citizen, and therefore entitled to enter the United States. But Japanese and Filipinos make up half the population of the archipelago. In short, it serves as a kind of 'lock' between over-populated Asia and prohibited America. A halt for one generation in these oceanic islands suffices to throw open the promised land.

This American creation, this port of call, this point of plantation, involves no forming of a nation. It means merely an aboriginal population in process of extinction, and a heterogeneous population coming into being which will take a long time to merge into a new race. The present-day interest of the colony is that it is a stage-point for American power on its way to Asia just as it is a stepping-stone where Asiatic emigrants set foot on their way to the New World.

THE PHILIPPINES

Unlike the Hawaiis, the great Philippine archipelago is both a State and a nation: a nation partly of European origin, with a centuries-old tradition of civilised life. This archipelago, off the coast of Asia, is an observation-post and a fortress of the American Republic.

To the west of Asia, the belt of islands around the continent spreads out in an immense arc off shore from Western China. Between Taiwan (Formosa) and Borneo, this arc is marked, like a dotted line, by the seven thousand and eighty-three islands of the Philippine archipelago. This number is misleading. Four thousand six hundred and forty-two of the islands do not even possess a name, and only four hundred and sixty-six of them have an area over a square mile or so. The two largest, Luzon and Mindanao, are respectively a little more and a little less than forty thousand square miles in area. They constitute two-thirds of the surface of the archipelago: one of the pleasantest of tropical lands.

Here lives a very old people. Apart from the last surviving aborigines – negroid dwarfs in the forests and the mountains – and the few barbarian tribes of the interior (not more than a million people), the Filipinos are a peaceful population made up of some ten million Malay farmers and fishermen, with a kind of aristocracy whose native blood is mixed with a percentage – sometimes a very high percentage – of Spanish or, more rarely, Chinese blood. Arab exploration has left half a million of Mohammedan Moros in Mindanao and the Sulu Islands; but the great social, religious and linguistic transformation of the islands followed the Spanish conquest.

It was not from Europe that the Spaniards came to the Philippines. From its very first contact with the Whites, the archipelago was set within an American sphere of influence. Magellan discovered it, in 1521, and he reached it by way of the Pacific, not the Indian Ocean. It was from Mexico that Legaspi set sail in 1565 to conquer the islands, where he established the first colonial administration at Cebu in 1575. From Acapulco he followed the Mexican coast, and then steered towards the west. The expeditions to the Philippines in the sixteenth century were a sequel to exploration on the west coast of America. Accordingly the Philippines became connected with New Spain: with the West Indies, not the East Indies. So one may say that the United States took over the same inheritance here as they did in the Gulf of Mexico and to the north of the Rio Grande del Norte.

Nevertheless, the reason why they went to the Philippines is not well known. In his *The United States as a World Power*, Professor Archibald C. Coolidge declares that the Washington Government 'never had the least intention of taking possession of the archipelago,' and that, as a humorist put it, the average American could not have said whether the Philippines were 'the name of an archipelago or the name of a jam.'

During the Spanish-American War, however, an American fleet happened to be at Hongkong. Since it could neither stay there nor go to any other neutral port, and since its return to American waters would have been regarded as a retreat, 'the only thing it could do was to seek out the enemy at their general headquarters': in other words, Manila. So the Philippines were conquered; and then the United States did not quite know what to do with them. 'The proof that the Government had no definite designs on the islands,' Professor Coolidge goes on, 'is that it had taken no steps to follow up its victory.'

If a handful of imperialists were proud to see their country become an Asiatic power, more level-headed statesmen would have been glad to get rid of the archipelago. But how could they ? Were they entitled to do so ? In other words, had not Providence specially chosen America upon this occasion ? Mr. Rudyard Kipling had just reminded Americans that they ought to bear their share of 'the white man's burden.' The descendants of the Pilgrim Fathers could have no doubt, in whole-hearted sincerity, that they had a duty to fulfil towards the Philippine people. Anyone who fails to understand this state of mind, or rather this case of conscience, will never really understand the history and policy of the peoples of British stock.

So, in 1898, the Americans found themselves face to

face with a task which was quite a novelty to them. The Philippines, with their fertile volcanic soil and their stout peasant population, were a fine country. But they were grovelling in squalor, sloth, and ignorance. Until 1834, Spain had treated the islands as a kind of China closed against foreign trade. The monks ruled the people with a heavy hand, and their territorial wealth was such that in the region of Manila alone they had more than sixty thousand farmers.

While the Americans were still engaged in suppressing the insurgents, who carried on against them the guerrilla warfare begun against the Spaniards, they immediately set about organising a police force; for bandits swarmed. Then they were fired with an enthusiasm for education and public health at which they themselves sometimes smiled. A member of the Taft Mission in 1906, Mr. A. Brownwell, related that one of his friends told him that his manservant had left him to turn student, and that what everybody was talking about at the moment was whether it was better to drink boiled water, distilled water, or mineral water. But the fact remains that, by as early as 1918, some 62 per cent of the Filipinos over ten years of age could read and write: a percentage which many a European country is still far from having reached.

Within thirty-five years, the Philippines have passed from the Middle Ages to the twentieth century. Public works, drainage, railways and other means of communication have been carried out. Manila, situated on the slow-flowing river Pasig, has preserved all the charm of old Spanish cities, and at the same time has developed into a capital with 341,000 inhabitants, possessing shady, scented parks side by side with modern factories. Thus the Philippines are at once modern and medieval, just as their climate is at once tropical and temperate.

Two sets of figures sum up their economic transformation. Foreign trade increased from a value of sixty-eight million pesos in 1899 to a maximum value of six hundred and twenty-three million in 1929: the world-crisis in 1931 reduced it to four hundred and six million. Sugar-cane products make up one-third of exports, and coco-nut products another third. Then come fibre-products, in the first place *abaca*, the famous Manila hemp; and finally tobacco, embroideries, forest products, fibre-hats, and that opaline mother-of-pearl in surprisingly large sheets which so prettily softens the tropical light out there – and here at home the glare of electric light. But the production of hemp is steadily declining. A score of years ago it constituted 57 per cent of exports, and sugar only 16 per cent. The change is not without its dangers in view of the world over-production of sugar, and of the possible closing of the American market.

On the other hand, the Filipinos produce neither their own clothes, their own tools, nor their own food. Cotton-goods stand at the head of the list of imports, followed by metallurgical products, rice (despite the fine rice-fields in the islands), wheat, flour and macaroni. These are not the marks of a very stable economic situation.

From the political point of view as well as the economic, it should be added that during the past thirty years 56 per cent of the total trade was done with the United States and Hawaii, and that in 1933 this percentage rose to 87, while Japan, who comes next, figured only to the extent of 7 per cent.

Thus a direct and very strong economic link has gradually been forged between the Philippines and the United States, which knew so little about one another a third of a century ago. The Americans are not only the archipelago's main providers, but also its best customers. Among its chief products, only hemp is exported mostly to Japan. Almost all its sugar, two-thirds of its copra, and nearly half its tobacco go to the United States, together with all its coco-nut oil and all its embroideries. Accordingly, the obstacle that would be presented by a prohibitive American customs tariff would mean an economic disaster for the Philippines.

From the political point of view, what would be the situation of the United States in the Far East if they abandoned Manila, which has been described as being to them what Hongkong is to Great Britain ? And what would be the repercussion of their departure upon Great Britain's position at Hongkong, in the Malay peninsula, and even in India; upon Holland's position in her Malay archipelago; and upon France's position in Indo-China ?

Side by side with their economic improvement, the Philippines have acquired both a desire for independence and a realisation that independence cannot be lasting unless it is preceded by political stability. The Filipino leaders are well aware that such stability has not yet been attained. A few years ago experiments in State Socialism brought the country, after it had prospered under American administration, within an ace of bankruptcy; and this misadventure made

Filipino politicians circumspect. Aguinaldo, the hero of the great struggle for independence, the man most beloved by the Malay peasants and most respected by everybody else, felt that collaboration between the two races should not yet come to an end. Senator Manuel Quezón, leader of the nationalist opposition, considered that there should be a transitional autonomous régime for ten years, after which a plebiscite should decide upon the permanent form of Filipino relations with the United States.

In the legislative sphere, the Jones Law of 1916 marked a decisive step in the direction of such a régime. It created a Senate and a Chamber elected by the people, while the Governor and the Ministers were nominated by the Washington Government. The Council of State was reduced to a consultative rôle, and the head of the justiciary remained, as he had been before, a Filipino. The resulting status of the Philippines was one which, in the British Empire, would be called intermediary between that of a Crown colony and that of a Dominion.

Between 1929 and 1932, several Bills were introduced in the United States Congress with the object of granting independence to the Philippines. The Hare-Hawes-Cutting Act, passed at the end of 1932, and upheld by Congress on January 17, 1933, despite President Hoover's veto, preserved American control over legislation and foreign affairs for a period of ten years. At the same time, it progressively closed the United States market to Filipino products and immigration into the United States to Filipino citizens. In addition, it stipulated that, even after the grant of independence, the United States should retain military and naval bases in the Philippines. The Filipino Parliament refused this gift, and the upshot was a recasting of parties at Manila into two groups, in accordance with their respective attitude towards the independence law: the 'Pros' and the 'Antis.'

In November 1933, Senator Quezón paid a visit to the United States with the object of obtaining more satisfactory conditions. After several months' negotiation, he secured elimination of the clause in connection with military and naval bases, and a promise of unconditional independence after a period of ten years. But otherwise, and especially in so far as the transitional period is concerned, the Tydings-McDuffie Bill recommended by President Roosevelt on March 2, 1934, and adopted by Congress almost at once, scarcely differs from the Act of 1933. It was presented to the Manila Parliament on May 1, 1934, and a year later, on May 14, 1935, the Filipino people, voting in the plebiscite which it stipulated, accepted it.

The consequent prospect of complete independence, however, arouses no enthusiasm in the archipelago. People who followed the process of lobbying in its favour at Washington allege that the Tydings-McDuffie Act is intended, before all else, to serve the interests of sugar-cane planters in Hawaii and the West Indies, beetroot farmers in the United States, American tobacco-growers and oil-producers, all of whom want to get rid of Filipino competition; and also to satisfy the American workers' unions, who are bent on checking Filipino immigration into Hawaii and the Western States.

The Filipinos are afraid of an economic crisis when they lose their chief customer and, in the case of some

commodities, their sole customer.[1]   They dread an in-
flux of Chinese labour.   They know that political dis-
turbances are likely to ensue, including a popular
agitation for the nationalisation, or the breaking-up,
of the immense estates which the Roman Catholic
Church still possesses in the archipelago.   They feel
that their main chance of economic salvation may
some day come from Japan, who already has a grip
on the hemp industry, and who recently offered to
buy all the Filipino sugar which might become available owing to the closing of the United States market.
But the Filipinos also realise that such economic assistance to them on Japan's part is quite likely to lead to
Japanese political intervention.   Incidentally, an unexpected upshot of the existing situation was that in 1934
China sent a commercial mission to the Philippines
and appointed a Minister in Manila.

If the United States wash their hands of the Philippines, it is unquestionable that the Filipinos will often
sigh for the flesh-pots of Egypt and for their sometime
state of 'servitude,' which lacked neither convenience
nor charm.   A time will come when old Filipinos will
tell their children that those who have not known the
era of American domination cannot realise what
sweetness of life means.   Nevertheless, the history of
the Philippines seems to be entering upon a new phase,
when the archipelago will become more and more
closely associated with the geographical and human
environment in which Nature placed it: an environment lit by the rays of the Rising Sun.

[1] Exports to United States in 1933= $93,048,000; imports from
United States in 1933= $44,782,000.

The United States and Tropical America

The political geography of tropical America, the isthmus countries and the Caribbean islands, not to speak of the southern part of the continent, is evolving before our eyes, if not with a continuous movement, at least in a constant direction.

A third of a century ago, the island part of this region, with the exception of Haiti and San Domingo, consisted of British, Danish, Spanish, French, and Dutch colonies. In the isthmus part of it, between Mexico at one extreme and Colombia at the other, were five republics and a small British colony. The continental part was occupied by republics and the three Guianas, French, Dutch, and British.

Now Spain has lost her colonies: Cuba has proclaimed herself a republic, and Porto-Rico has become American. Denmark has sold her islands to the United States, which call them the Virgin Islands. The Panama Canal Zone is American, and the State surrounding it is a republic created under the aegis of the United States. What is not shown on the map, moreover, is the economic and even political influence of the United States which has persisted since their military or financial occupation of San Domingo, Haiti, and Nicaragua, and the control of Honduras by a powerful American commercial company engaged in the fruit trade. All these changes have a common characteristic : the Americanisation, in different degrees, of certain parts of the islands and the isthmus. This evolution, with its variety, recalls the evolution, with a similar variety, of the Asiatic States bordering on India.

This is not the effect of a sudden tendency towards colonial expansion on the part of a country which refused to commit itself to overseas adventures for so long that, less than a century ago, geography text-books, after enumerating the European colonies in their chapter on the Pacific, added evasively: 'The United States also possess a few islands.' At the outset of the Spanish-American War, the Washington Government proclaimed that Cuba should be free, and later it showed no hurry, and, above all, no doctrinaire spirit, in going to the Philippines.

The allegedly imperialist policy of the United States in the Central American isthmus and the West Indies is, in fact, much more bound up with the organisation of what may be called the Republic's metropolitan territory than with any such thing as imperialism or pan-Americanism. The Panama Canal, which shortens the sea-route from New York to San Francisco by nearly seven thousand miles, and whose attraction for trade is unaffected by the transcontinental railways, plays in American economy the rôle of an interior route, just as the Suez Canal does in the economy of the British Empire.

As soon as the Spanish *conquistadores* set eyes on the Pacific, they started searching for a means of maritime communication by way of the isthmus between the east and west parts of the Spanish empire. They dreamed of a canal across the isthmus of Tehuantepec, or fol-lowing the great north-south cleft in Honduras. The gold-seekers of 1848, in order to get from the east of the United States to California without either making the almost impossible attempt to cross the continent, or embarking on the long and dangerous voyage round

South America, took the short cut which Nature freely offered to adventurous men. They shipped to the San Juan river, went up it, crossed the Nicaraguan lakes, and, after a short and easy march, reached the Pacific, where coasting vessels were always available to sail to California. For, if the crossing of the isthmus was longer here than elsewhere, nowhere was it more easy.

Accordingly, the first plans for cutting a canal in the nineteenth century adopted this itinerary. It was the Panama route, however, which carried the day. Means were found for getting the American Government to take over the ill-fated French enterprise, with the result that the American Government cut the canal and created an isthmian republic, a twofold territorial margin protecting the 'Canal Zone,' over which floats the Stars and Stripes. Such was the birth of Panama, at once a work of art on a national route of the United States and the shortest way towards the markets of the Pacific coast of South America.

If we return to the West Indian 'Mediterranean,' what we see there is the crystallisation, in their modern form, of the natural relations between North America and tropical America. I say 'North America,' not merely the United States; for the new relations between Canada and the British West Indies throw perhaps the best light on this interdependence. These Caribbean islands, together with British Guiana, are the chief providers, within the British Empire, of the northern Dominion, apart from Great Britain herself. India is only half as important, and Australia only one-third as important. But the islands are as yet only secondary customers of Canada.

In other words, in accordance with the natural order of things tropical America is becoming more and more complementary to North America. It provides North America with its agricultural products, its forest and mineral raw material; and, so far as its wealth and population permit, it buys manufactured products from North America.

The outstanding features in the political geography of these isthmian and island States are their excessive political division – their area varies from Salvador's 13,176 square miles to Nicaragua's 51,660 square miles – and their scanty population. Cuba, the most densely populated, has 3,600,000 inhabitants; Haiti 2,300,000; Guatemala 2,000,000; and all the others from 450,000 to 900,000. Even in South America, the entirely tropical republics, with territories more extensive than those of the largest European States, number only from 700,000 inhabitants to 6,000,000. Their demographic average is about that of the new Baltic States.

It should be added that not all of these countries, whose ethnographic composition is very complex, have as yet attained political stability and financial security. Though they are lands of immense natural wealth, their development can be undertaken only with capital from outside. Their internal situation and their material weakness mean that such capital demands guarantees of security, which·may go so far as direct intervention in their political life by the authority that organises their economic life.

So political relations have developed which could be represented on the map only by means of a range of carefully graded tints. After the Panama Canal Zone, the variety of the countries in tropical America which are satellites of the United States begins with the American colonies, properly speaking, of Porto-Rico and the Virgin Islands. Then come the States which are independent, but were created by the Americans: the republics of Cuba and Panama. Finally, over independent States of longer standing, the United States have exercised, or still exercise, supervision in one form or another: financial control in Haiti; fiscal control in San Domingo; American *gendarmerie* in Haiti; protection by American marines of American interests in Nicaragua, where, in addition, American naval bases are contemplated in the Corn Islands and in Fonseca Bay if the projected Nicaraguan canal is constructed. One may also recall the case of Honduras, which is mediatised under the authority of an American fruit company.

This list, however, is not exhaustive, either geographically or politically. For that matter, in one and the same country the type of control or occupation has varied from time to time. Moreover, it is not without interest to note that, even before the economic crisis became acute in 1933 – in other words, during a period of prosperity – a marked diminution in United States intervention in the affairs of the little West Indian and isthmian republics was already to be observed. But it would be very rash to interpret this as implying any radical change in the external policy of the United States.

Little by little, the American tropical world is becoming organised. Interesting parallels might be drawn with tropical Africa, and above all with tropical Asia. But we should be in danger of making a grave mistake if we overlooked the fact that, while

Nature has created spontaneous relations between North America and tropical America, another pole of geographical attraction is to be found in the south in the great States belonging to the same civilisation, almost all speaking the same language, and, with one exception, having at least part of their territory in the tropics. It would be an interesting subject of study to consider which of the two attractions will prove the stronger, and how their respective actions and reactions may gradually modify the political map of tropical America.

VIII

TERRITORIES AND FRONTIERS
IN SOUTH AMERICA

COLONIAL FRONTIERS AND YOUNG REPUBLICS

THE settlement of South American territorial conflicts is one of the great anxieties of the League of
Nations. A single episode of these conflicts, the dispute between Bolivia and Paraguay over Fort Vanguardia, in 1928, is said to have cost the League
twenty-eight thousand dollars in telegrams; for, if
our day does not attain its objects more rapidly than
did the diplomats of Hellas and Troy, it loves to per-
suade itself that it pursues them with wonderful speed.

In the case either of the Chaco conflict, three-
quarters of a century old, or of some sudden clash
between Colombia and Peru on the Upper Amazon,
Europeans are equally astounded at the passion which
the combatants bring to the dispute. This is because
they are inclined to regard such disputes merely as
local episodes, concerned with something like carving
out the frontiers of new States in quite virgin soil.

On the contrary, these South American frontiers are
almost as laden with history as our own, and they are
pregnant with a future no less disturbing and even
more uncertain. When they won their independence
a century ago, the young republics adopted, more or

less provisionally, the divisions of the old Spanish colonial viceroyalties, *audiencias, capitanías* and *intendencias*. Since then cruel wars and successive treaties have modified these frontiers. But, whether it is a question of transferring a 'march' or quibbling about a frontier-line, one is dealing simultaneously with a *limes* – a time-honoured frontier, traced and described on parchment with more than apparent precision in the pompous terms of old royal decrees – and with frontier-zones: those hotbeds for thorny subjects of conflict.

We must therefore bear in mind that the data of political geography in South America are very different from European data. Otherwise we are very prone to exaggerate the importance of some of them, and, still more, to underestimate the importance of certain capital ones.

One of the main sources of error in studying the politics of these countries is that there is no break in continuity between their *metropolitan* territory proper and a kind of *colonial* territory. By a series of almost imperceptible transitions, the zone of civilised and relatively dense population, of great cities which have nothing to envy Europe, of intensively cultivated fields, is succeeded by primeval forest and bush, where rival pioneers meet and clash, hoisting their respective flags over the territory of scattered, nomadic, and often quite savage natives. In these out-of-the-way places, incidents occur which recall European colonial conflicts in the nineteenth century, and perhaps the combats on the confines of the Empires of Rome and Charlemagne.

But it also happens that something which, from the

first dispatches, looks like simply a colonial frontier incident proves, on investigation, to be a serious territorial question, involving the metropolitan part of the republic concerned. It may be a conflict such as that over Leticia, a quarrel about a *hacienda* in the bush, which was successfully localised; or it may be a conflict such as that over the Chaco, an historic dispute which goes so far back as the sixteenth-century Spanish kings and calls them as witnesses in a matter involving the life or death of a present-day republic.

COLOMBIA AND PERU ON THE UPPER AMAZON

During the night of September 1, 1932, a party of Peruvians crossed the Amazon, entered Colombia, attacked the village of Leticia, imprisoned the authorities, hauled down the Colombian flag, replaced it by that of Peru, and declared the territory 'restored' to the Peruvian Republic. The Lima Government promptly disavowed their action; but local movements at Iquitos made the Government reconsider its attitude. The result was that this raid led to a war, which might have gone on for a long time but for the intervention of the League of Nations in February and March 1933.

At the time of the revolutionary movement for independence from Spain, the frontier between the viceroyalties of New Granada and Peru was adopted in principle by the central republic from which emerged Venezuela, Colombia, and Ecuador. This frontier ran in the little-known region of the Upper Amazon: that river, comparable in South America with the Great Lakes in North America, up which sea-going ships can proceed from the Atlantic to the foot of the

Andes, to the Colombian frontier, and to the very heart of Peru.

Owing to this importance of the Amazon, Colombia insisted that her frontier should reach its course at some point. This was agreed upon by the treaty which was signed at Lima, in 1922, by Señor Salomón on behalf of Peru, and Señor Lazano on behalf of Colombia, approved by the Colombian Congress in 1925, and by the Peruvian Congress in 1927, ratified and promulgated by the presidents of the two States, and officially registered with the League of Nations in 1928. This treaty laid down that the frontier between Colombia and Peru should be the river Putumayo to the point where the Yahuas flows into it; then a line running southwards to the junction of the Atauari and the Amazon; and finally the *thalweg* of the Amazon to Leticia, where the frontier joined the Tabatinga-Apaporis line, the old frontier between Brazil and Peru according to the treaty of 1851, which was confirmed at the end of 1928 by a treaty between Colombia and Brazil.

Let us now recall Colombia's geographical situation. Though she has a lengthy Atlantic coast-line and also a Pacific coast-line, which was uninhabited until the opening of the Panama Canal, at the same time she is not one of those countries where coastal settlement gradually spreads inland. The Andes extend across her from south-west to north in three ranges, in between which the rivers Magdalena and Cauca flow to the Atlantic. Colombia's centres of life and activity are on the inland plateaux, with their perpetual spring. Here flourishes Bogota, the capital, in a region where whites and Indians – the latter being descendants of

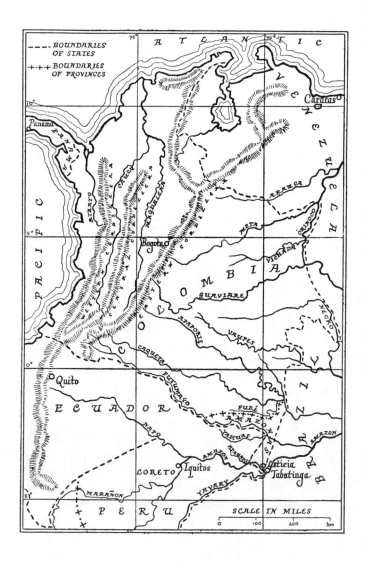

the highly civilised Chibchas – intermarry in the lower classes. Here is the district of Antioquia, wholly Spanish, whose population is increasing at one of the most rapid rates in South America. The provinces are no mere administrative units in a new country: they remind one of the provinces of France or Spain, and have their own individuality and their own highly differentiated human types. Such is Andean Colombia.

But to the east extend the savannahs, the *llanos*, the Amazonian forest, which constitute, so to speak, a colonial extension of this metropolitan Colombia. The left-bank tributaries of the Orinoco flow across it almost parallel from west to east: the Arauca, which forms the frontier with Venezuela, the Meta, the Vichada, and the Guaviare. Then come the left-bank tributaries of the Upper Amazon, and their tributaries in turn: the Vaupes; the Caqueta, swollen by the Apaporis and the Putumayo, which separates Colombia on the south from Ecuador and Peru. Most of the administrative divisions of these immense territories – in the west of which mission settlements flourished in the eighteenth century – bear the names of the sole constant entities in them, namely the rivers; and the rare villages – centres of grazing or forest exploitation – are not far away from the rivers, especially the Vichada and the Putumayo.

To the south of the river Puré as far as the Putumayo and in the trapezoid area between the Putumayo and the Amazon, the Colombian Government, as a sequel to the Salomón–Lazano Treaty, which recognised its right to this territory, created the national *Intendencia* of Amazonas, with Leticia as its capital and its port

on the Amazon. In 1931, Leticia was nothing more
than a hamlet of some thirty huts with thatched roofs.
It had no public buildings of any kind, and no road
linked it with the rest of the world. Colombia set to
work actively. She dispatched officials, engineers, and
capital, constructed wireless-telegraphy pylons, built
a town hall, a school, and a church, and started roads
towards several little centres, which she also began
organising. The main undertaking was the making of
a river port, at which timber, rubber, and balata-gum
could be loaded straight on to sea-going ships.

Grazing will doubtless become a great industry in
this region. The conflict in September 1932 appears
to have had its origin in an unsuccessful attempt on the
part of some Peruvians to sell a *hacienda* to Colombia:
a highly coloured story which, whatever may be the
truth about it, at least demonstrates the possible importance of agricultural development in the region.

Though whites are few in the savannahs and the
forests of the Orinoco and the Amazon, their nationality does not lack variety. In the *llanos* of western
Colombia travel Venezuelan pedlars, who follow the
rivers by boat and the tracks with their pack-mules.
The non-Indian population of the *intendencia* of
Amazonas is made up of Colombians, Peruvians, and
Brazilians. So it is obvious how easily little local
incidents may turn into diplomatic conflicts.

The Peruvian district of Loreto appears to have
developed the mentality of a frontier province. Testi-
mony was borne to this during the Leticia dispute by
reports of manifestations at Iquitos, its capital. Brazil
– whose Fort Tabatinga marks the meeting-point of
the Brazilian, Colombian, and Peruvian frontiers –

knows where the danger lies. At the beginning of September 1932, the *Diario de Noticias* of Rio de Janeiro reminded the Government that the Brazilian forts on the frontiers of the Upper Amazon were falling into ruin, and declared that it was urgent to rebuild them.

A quotation from the Lima newspaper, *El Comercio*, will convey some idea of the way in which national passions sometimes complicate even statistical study of these regions. On November 1, 1932, this paper wrote: 'The territory of Leticia is a Peruvian territory of more than forty thousand square miles peopled by seventeen thousand inhabitants, all of them Peruvians.' According to Colombian documents, however, Peruvians number only about five hundred in the whole *intendencia* of Amazonas, which, moreover, covers only some eight thousand square miles. One is reminded of a philosopher's saying: that argument would be remarkably facilitated – and would sometimes, indeed, prove unnecessary – if people began by agreeing about the meaning of the terms they used.

But at least the intervention of the League of Nations had a happy issue. The voyage of nearly five thousand miles made by a squadron of small Colombian war-ships, which set off from Carthagena on the estuary of the Amazon and went up the river to Leticia, showed what efforts Colombia was prepared to make to keep the territory – recognised as hers by the treaty with Peru – which gave her a port on the great river. The League of Nations persuaded the belligerents to sign an agreement on May 25, 1933, and on the following June 25 a League of Nations Commission arrived in the territory in dispute for the purpose of administering it provisionally, with the co-operation of the Colombian army. Almost exactly a year later, a definite treaty of peace was signed at Rio de Janeiro, and the territory was restored to Colombia.

The treaty was not finally ratified by the Bogota Parliament until July 1935; but the reason for this delay wholly concerned Colombian internal politics. On the preceding February 7, the Senate, in which the Conservative opposition had a majority, refused to follow the Chamber's example in ratifying the treaty. This, however, was purely a question of form, and had no effect on the relations between the two countries.

The point about this episode that we must especially bear in mind is that the fixing of a frontier in South America is something quite different from drawing a geodesic line in the midst of an uninhabited region which has hitherto been *res nullius*. The Amazon, like a South American Mediterranean, attracts all the neighbouring peoples. Colombia has won her case; but Ecuador has not yet settled the line of her frontier between the river Napo and the Putumayo. Little by little, the political map of the Upper Amazon region is being drawn; it is based on geographical and human factors which were scarcely taken into account in the first divisions of the continent transcribed on their rough maps by the cartographers of the *conquistadores*.

The Northern Chaco

The Gran Chaco, to the south-east of Bolivia, is a plain several times the size of France, which extends from the river system of the Rio de la Plata to the eastern buttresses of the Andes, and from the Argentine Pampa to the plains of the Upper Amazon. The

Southern Chaco, from the river Salado to the Bermajo, and the Central Chaco, between the Bermajo and the Pilcomayo, are Argentine. The Northern Chaco, to the north of the Pilcomayo, is Bolivian ; but it is claimed, at least partly, by Paraguay. Such were the cause and the setting of the war which, from 1932 to 1935, set the armies of the Andean republic and the riverain republic at grips—just as their diplomats had been for the past eighty years – and puzzled the legists of the League of Nations: to no great purpose.

The Chaco is a flat, dreary tropical savannah, which descends slowly from an altitude of some three thousand feet at the foot of the Andes to a minimum altitude of about two hundred feet on the river Paraguay. The temperature, which may go as high as 108° in the shade when the hot, humid north wind blows, falls below 32° when the icy *zurazo* from the south blows across the pampa, with no obstacle to stop it all the way from Patagonia.

The interior of the Northern Chaco, little known and almost uninhabited, is flooded from November to April by overflowed streams. During dry weather, these streams dwindle away into sands, and their surface, flush with the plain, is still as that of a pond. During the floods, the few elevations become so many islands, where the animals of the savannah take refuge. When the water recedes, in every depression it leaves a pestilential pool, swarming with mosquitoes, and with flocks of marsh birds hovering over it.   It is a land of fever, where even the Indians rarely venture. Since total drought alternates with floods of rain, nothing grows in this soil – a clay substratum covered by sand, with brackish, salty water-courses – except brushwood

and prickly shrubs.   But the land is not entirely barren.
On the least favoured side of it, which is the side towards the Pilcomayo, cattle-breeding is possible, and

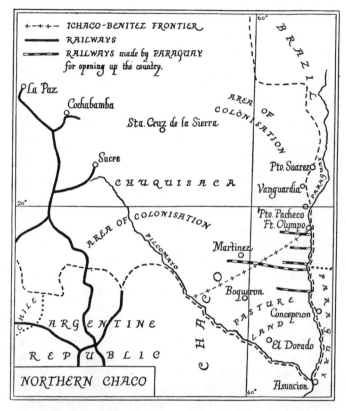

scientific farming could regulate the water-supply,
organise cultivation, and develop ranching, which
would lead to agricultural industries.

This inhospitable savannah is hemmed by tropical

forest with a magnificent green border sixty miles wide. On the right bank of the Paraguay, and in some of the western regions, in the neighbourhood of Santa Cruz de la Sierra, the spontaneous fertility of the soil is wonderful. The forest abounds in valuable timber and medicinal plants. In the first rank among these trees is the red iron-wood, the *quebracho rojo*, the 'red axe-breaker,' which never rots. Its bark is so rich in tannin that the Argentine Republic annually exports about one hundred and seventy-five thousand tons of tannic acid from its Chaco and the province of Santa Fé, while in 1931 Paraguay exported about thirty-six thousand tons of *quebracho* extract from the Northern Chaco.

With the forest alternates grazing-land. Oil-bearing land has been found, and the Standard Oil Company has bored sixteen wells. The potential wealth of this territory, which, so far as its centre is concerned, is one of the most unpleasant in the world, is considerable. But – except in the Argentine part of it, the Southern Chaco, with which we are not here concerned – its development is still very backward.

Since for years past Bolivia's history has been so tragic that she might be called a South American Poland, the country has retired within itself. The Bolivians – Spaniards, Quichuas, and Aymaras – are a race of mountaineers, accustomed to the almost cold climate of high altitudes and unattracted by the tropical marshes of the river region. The part of the Chaco nearest to the Andes Mountains is the roughest. The banks of the Pilcomayo, the first sphere of action which presented itself to the Bolivians, are far from comparable with the right bank of the Paraguay.

Finally, nobody offered Bolivian enterprise the capital necessary for the development of the Chaco, where Bolivian economic activity has always been limited.

On the contrary, from their capital Asunción and their other cities on the river Paraguay, San Pedro and Concepción, the Paraguayans had as their western horizons the magnificent tropical woodland on the other side of the river. So the Chaco struck them by its wealth and beauty. Paraguayan woodcutters, Guarani Indians, willingly worked in its forest belt, where the extraction of tannin from *quebracho* became so lucrative an industry during the European war that, in order to exploit the forest, several narrow-gauge railways were constructed, with their tracks perpendicular to the river; in one case penetrating one hundred and twenty-five miles into the Chaco.

These enterprises were undertaken on concessions granted by Paraguay to foreign companies, mostly Argentine, as is shown by a map recently published in Buenos Aires. In short, while the war was in progress Paraguay had already ceded most of the Chaco to foreign capitalists, though the Asunción Government represented the Chaco to the world as national territory for which the Paraguayan people were ready to fight to the last gasp.

THE CONFLICT BETWEEN BOLIVIA AND PARAGUAY

All this might lead one to ask whether a region like this did not remain *res nullius*, and whether Paraguay has not acquired rights of first occupancy in it. On the contrary, this territory has been the subject-matter of title-deeds for centuries past.

Bolivia has presented diplomats and jurisconsults

with documentation going back to the beginning of the colonial period. This documentation is all the more important because, at the outset of their independence,

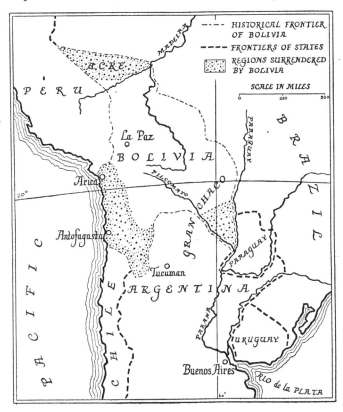

the young South American republics determined the extent of their respective domains, in accordance with the old colonial divisions, by the *uti possidetis juris* of 1810. Bolivia thus became the successor-State of the former *audiencia* of Charcas, the Spanish colonial capital of Upper Peru, later known as La Plata, and then as Sucre. Now to this judicial, administrative, and political division successive royal decrees (*cedulas*) between the sixteenth and the eighteenth centuries, had assigned the Chaco. This, moreover, was one of the cases where boundaries were clearly defined, for the river Paraguay was specifically mentioned. The river thus became the eastern frontier of Bolivia, just as it had been the frontier of the colonial units which that republic replaced.

In 1843, however, the republic of Paraguay began to think about extending to the west. It commenced by claiming possession of the whole width of the river Paraguay, thus paving the way for annexation on the right bank. On that bank, in fact, in 1855, about twenty miles upstream from Asunción, the Paraguayans founded the town of Nuevo Burdeos, now known as Villa Hayes. In 1888 the Paraguayan gunboat *Pirapo* went up the river to the neighbourhood of the twentieth degree of latitude – in other words, between the Brazilian and the Bolivian banks – and seized the Bolivian port of Puerto Pacheco. Meanwhile the Asunción Government was putting territorial concessions in the Bolivian Chaco up for auction in the Buenos Aires market.

As a result, the two republics of Bolivia and Paraguay were not the only ones concerned. Morgenstern's map, drawn up between 1846 and 1858 and dedicated to the Paraguayan Congress, bore a tasteful observation on the right bank of the river between the 25th and the 26th degrees of latitude, not far from the inscription: 'Republic of Bolivia.' This observation read: '*Chaco paraguayo ocupado por fuerzas argentinas.*'

Bolivia had been weakened by war, and, according to Bolivian writers themselves, by the mistakes of certain of her statesmen. She had already been compelled to cede her Pacific coast provinces to Chile and Peru, and, later, the Central Chaco to the Argentine, and the territory of the Acre to Brazil. She now agreed to share the Northern Chaco with Paraguay. By a series of treaties, she surrendered regions more and more extensive: 4,316 square leagues in 1879; 4,808 in 1887; 5,226 in 1894; and, finally, 9,124 in 1907.

Oddly enough, Paraguay never ratified any of these treaties, advantageous to her though they were. But she established herself on the right bank of the river Paraguay, where she organised military occupation, and sold concessions to foreign companies. In the marshy plain, Paraguayan and Bolivian forts came to be built: regular colonial outposts in the bush, most of them mere palisaded enclosures, with quarters for a few score of soldiers and their officers, stables, and out-houses. So, little by little, an armed frontier was constituted: a truly suitable skirmishing ground.

The frontiers of the successive 'treaties' between Bolivia and Paraguay were either two straight lines intersecting at right angles, one of them running from west to east and ending on the river Paraguay, and the other running from north to south and ending on the river Pilcomayo; or else a single straight line, running from one river to the other in such a way as to form a triangle, whose angles were the confluence of the two rivers and the points where the frontier touched them. Most of the maps now in common use in Europe mark the frontier fixed by the Ichaco-Benitez Treaty. This line starts from the Pilcomayo a little to the south of the 23rd degree of latitude, and ends at the point where the river Paraguay intersects the 21st degree. It is a line which, geographically, is perhaps the least absurd out of all this frontier-making on paper.

On the eve of the Fort Vanguardia incident, the line of Bolivian forts followed the Pilcomayo to the 24th parallel, then ran due north, and linked up with the forts constructed on the Paraguay to the south of Puerto Suarez. The Paraguayans had built their forts along a kind of horseshoe line from El Dorado through Boqueron to Martinez, and on the river Paraguay to the north of Puerto Pacheco.

During the night of December 5, 1928, the garrison of Fort Vanguardia, situated far beyond this Paraguayan line and in definitely Bolivian territory, was surprised and annihilated by a Paraguayan raiding force. The League of Nations managed to avoid an outbreak of war, and sentenced Paraguay to rebuild the fort. But in July 1932 there was another Paraguayan act of aggression in the region of Lake Chuquisaca. This marked the beginning of a series of raids on forts, attacks and counter-attacks. Little by little, these operations became transformed into a regular war, for which the two countries finally mobilised all their forces.

In the military sphere, it goes without saying, this war was conditioned by the same factors that characterised political, diplomatic, and economic activity in connection with the Northern Chaco for the past three-quarters of a century. On the one hand was the river-republic, situated in the neighbourhood, with a population accustomed to life in the savannah and the tropical forest. On the other hand was the Andean republic, compelled to provide its army with arms, munitions, supplies, and material by lines of communication hundreds of miles long which were barely practicable; and its army suffered terribly from a climate so different from that of the high plateaux.

The war went on for three years. During all this time, in the forests and the marshes of the Chaco, men were killed, or died of sickness and hardship, in the firm conviction that they were sacrificing their lives for a great national cause. Meanwhile at Geneva, at Washington, at Montevideo, representatives of the League of Nations and the neutral American States sought in vain for a formula capable of reconciling the interests, both obvious and obscure, which had set the Chaco on fire.

Finally, on June 12, 1935, an agreement between Paraguay and Bolivia was signed at Buenos Aires. It entrusted delegates of the Argentine, Brazil, Chile, and Uruguay, and also of the United States, with the task of reaching a settlement. If they failed to do so, the dispute was to be referred to The Hague Tribunal.

Rarely has any negotiation thrown into higher relief a conflict involving long-established title-deeds, lapsed treaties, modern tendencies, political and economic influences, avowed interests and occult intrigues. So the real origin of this conflict is worthy of investigation in the light of political geography.

THE REAL FACTORS IN THE CONFLICT

Side by side with juridical factors, which are usually the only ones taken into account, analysis of this conflict reveals psychological factors by no means to be neglected. Above all, however, it reveals economic factors and a problem of political geography. These have been left rather too much in the shade.

In the eyes of many people, the juridical argument suffices to explain the conflict, and even to settle it. If this were really the case, the issue would soon be decided; and, as one at least of the two parties would refuse to accept the verdict, the war would go on indefinitely – as, for that matter, it long looked like doing.

Bolivia, basing her case on royal decrees, the *uti possidetis juris*, and various arbitration awards and treaties, regards herself as successor-State and heiress to the *audiencia* of Charcas, whose territory included the Northern Chaco; accordingly the Northern Chaco is Bolivian. This thesis has very strong grounds in its favour.

On the other hand, there is no denying that the argument which Paraguay sets up against it seems casuistical, to say the least. One feels that it does not convince even the Paraguayans themselves. In his pamphlet, *Paraguay against Bolivia*, published in 1928, one of their higher officers, Major Samaniego, wrote: 'Our plan of war is the offensive in strategy and tactics. It is for us to choose the moment most favourable from the point of view of our campaign. When we have chosen this moment, our jurists and diplomats will undertake the task of justifying our conduct in the international sphere, in accordance with Machiavelli's wise maxims.' In short, the Paraguayan republic regards juridical factors in the same light as a certain King of Prussia, who could always be sure of finding some learned pedant to justify his annexations.

At the same time, the strength of these factors has been weakened by successive surrenders on the part of Bolivia herself. If Bolivia holds the Chaco territory by title of old royal decrees, Paraguay is in possession of treaties signed by Bolivian statesmen in the nineteenth century which cede her part of this territory. To be sure, the fact that a State, during a period of weakness, has voluntarily surrendered one province does not give anybody the right to deprive her of another by force: but such a thing often happens. Everybody knows to what an extent, in such cases, juridical ground seems to consist of shifting sands and becomes a world of fallacy and unreality.

Psychological elements convey this impression even more strongly. When the Asunción Government, in January 1934, refused to sign a two weeks' armistice, and pleaded that the Paraguayan people would not tolerate it, that Government may very well have been speaking the truth. When the La Paz Government declared that no Bolivian Government would survive the surrender of the Chaco for twenty-four hours, it is quite possible that it was not exaggerating either. The two peoples had been led to regard this war as a national war, and there is no doubt that they did so regard it. That, however, did not necessarily mean that this was its true character. It simply indicated the existence of a sentimental state of mind which must be taken into account. But to recognise the existence of this state of mind did not in itself suggest any solution, short of a war of extermination.

The economic constituent elements in the problem, for their part, are comparatively simple. To both the republics the Chaco represents considerable material value; but this value is of a different kind, and at a different phase of evolution, from their respective points of view. Both States regard the Chaco as a region where cattle-breeding, agriculture, and extractive industries may some day support a wholly new population; but this population has first to be brought into being, for Paraguayans and Bolivians will have plenty to do for some time to come in developing their uncontested territory. Moreover, nothing of the kind can be accomplished without foreign financial assistance, and the crisis has so far made any such assistance out of the question.

On the other hand, there are present possibilities. For Paraguay, the riverain Chaco is a region of timber land already being worked, and of agricultural industries in course of establishment. It can give employment to the republic's population of Guarani natives accustomed to tropical marshes; but, in the absence of Paraguayan capital, it can be developed only by foreign companies. For Bolivia, the Chaco is an historical heritage. Her mountaineers can work there only with difficulty. It is in the nature of a 'colony,' with its subsoil barely explored, though oil-wells have already been bored. It is a region which properly equipped companies could exploit to advantage.

For both sides, however, the Chaco is of value, most of all, on account of its geographical position. Its proximity arouses the desire of the Paraguayans, in possession of the left bank of the river Paraguay. The Bolivians regard it as their river domain and their antechamber to the Atlantic, giving them a seaport to take the place of those they lost half a century ago.

BOLIVIAN ACCESS TO THE SEA

For the essential feature of the Bolivian State is that it is a republic which politics, not Nature, have enclosed in its mountains, and that it yearns for the sea just as a prisoner yearns for freedom.

Until 1882, the year when the cruel war with Chile which cost her her maritime provinces came to an end, Bolivia, like all the other Andean States, had an outlet on the Pacific. Her nitrate coast from Antofagasta to Arica, apart from the intrinsic value of its manures, added national ports to the country's economic equipment and saved both imported goods and exported produce the cost of a long journey over foreign railways. What reason would Bolivia have had, then, to seek an Atlantic outlet to the east by a very roundabout river route? Between Santa Cruz de la Sierra, the most easterly town of the Andean region, and Puerto Suarez, the nearest point to the river Paraguay, lay nearly four hundred miles of rough country, almost without means of communication. Puerto Pacheco was of merely local importance. The sluggish Pilcomayo drowses along eleven hundred miles away from the plateau, separated from it by a marshy region, which means walking up to one's waist in water in order to attain the head-waters of the river's navigable reach, some one hundred and fifty miles above its confluence with the Paraguay.

To-day the Pilcomayo and the Paraguay constitute Bolivia's sole route, by way of a river which is not yet internationalised, but may become so, to the sea, which she must reach at all costs; for the railway from La Paz to Buenos Aires *viâ* Tucuman is slow for travellers and costly for goods. A pipe-line must also be constructed, for without it Bolivian oil is not worth much more in reservoirs than at the bottom of the wells; and that pipe-line must end on the quays of the great River Plate.

Such are the elements in the Chaco's economic value to the republic of Bolivia: a position value rather than an intrinsic value: a modern value, a future value, with an historical value in addition.

The historical and juridical basis of this value, the essential foundation of everything else, is the territory of the former *audiencia* of Charcas. Bolivia has undergone a process not of evolution, but of dissolution – a process frequent in political geography – and has been crumbling away at all her corners. Here it was a question not of a process of internal political dissolution gradually exhausting the country as a whole, but of a process of dissolution from outside destroying essential organs, especially that organ of communication most necessary to a State: its sea-coast. Geographical analysis shows that the Chaco is a substitute – imperfect, no doubt, but still capable of use – for Bolivia's lost coast. It is for this reason that Bolivia must retain it at all costs.

In this struggle, therefore, the Chaco, distant though it may be, tropical though it may be, inhospitable to the Quichuan mountaineers though it may be, is nevertheless for the Bolivians a national territory, essential to the life of the country. On the other hand, for the Paraguayans, Guaranis of the river, though the Chaco close to them resembles their own country, it is nevertheless a kind of colonial extension, a mere source of income, leased or sold to foreigners. It increases

Paraguay's wealth; but the very life of the country does not depend upon it.

Once this is understood, much that at first sight looks incoherent becomes clear: in the first place, the change in Bolivia's policy from her treaties surrendering the Chaco, to her construction of a line of forts to defend it. This line, in fact, is much more than the chain of blockhouses in the bush shown on local maps. It marks the limit of the minimum extent of national territory: the limit short of which the republic cannot live a normal economic life. Inland though it is, this Chaco frontier is a regular 'Atlantic coast' for Bolivia.

For this reason, Bolivia's sacrifice, if she admitted Paraguay's pretensions to the Chaco, would not be comparable with her sacrifice of hevea forests in the Acre territory in 1903. It would mean for her a dismembering like that of 1882, when Chile took her maritime provinces from her. She would lose not only her *quebracho* forests, her oil-wells, her future mines, her prairies and fields of to-morrow. She would also lose her second sea-lung – having already lost one – and her total asphyxiation would be merely a matter of time. So, when we study Bolivia of to-day, we are inevitably reminded of Poland.

Intervention of every kind, notably that of the other American republics, makes it more than doubtful whether such a fate will overtake her. We may assume that a satisfactory settlement will be made, and that a new life will soon begin for Bolivia. This new life of hers will possess an exceptional interest for the geographer.

Fifty years ago Bolivia, the heart of South America,

had three outlets to the sea: the Amazon, the river
Paraguay, and the Pacific coast. The first two, however, were at the end of such long corridors that she
scarcely thought of making use of them. An Andean
State, no doubt, but also a Pacific State: such was
Bolivia. Now the vicissitudes of her history compel
her to become an Atlantic State.

This remaking of the politico-geographical map
along lines which are, so to speak, anti-physical regis-
ters a most remarkable reversal of the country's
physical aptitudes. In order to go on living, this
Andean republic must make itself fluvial: not by con-
quering fresh territory, but by turning to account a
region of its ancestral domain which it had all but
abandoned, but which has now become invaluable to
it. This task will require courage and perseverance.
It has already involved Bolivia in years of war against
Paraguay. It will also require strong financial backing;
for hitherto Argentine interests have given Bolivia to
understand that they will never allow her to construct
a pipe-line from her oil-wells to the River Plate.

.   .   .   .

In short, a frontier in South America is quite a
different thing from a simple geometrical line drawn
through the bush in accordance with the arrangements
made in a diplomatic document. It is not even merely
a cartographical transcription of a juridical text. It
is something more than simply a division of territory
supposedly more or less rich. It is all this at one and
the same time; and, besides, it is a delimitation of the
realms of nations not according to the whims of men,
but according to the mutual reactions of mankind

and the earth. For this reason, neither ostentatious victories of force nor placid subtleties of law can ever in themselves settle these frontiers. Their settlement calls for a close study of politico-geographical organisms, which cannot be mutilated with impunity.

IX

THE POLAR REGIONS ENTER DIPLOMACY

NORTH ATLANTIC LIFE IN DAYS OF OLD

AT the Paris Colonial Exhibition in 1931, amid palatial buildings recalling tropical houses and landscapes, the general public – to whom the word 'colony' connotes 'hot country' – were surprised to find the home of the Queen of Snows: the pavilion of Greenland, the Danish Polar colony. In this Arctic creation they were delighted to discover all the features, and all the attraction, of great colonial achievements.

A little later, the world's attention was again directed to Greenland. This time, The Hague Tribunal was called upon to decide a dispute between two Scandinavian nations: a dispute representing two types of Polar colonisation. Norway claimed from Denmark a part of Greenland.

So people of our own time came to realise that the Polar regions do more than offer opportunities for fine feats of adventurous exploration and daring scientific expeditions. A whole new world made its entrance into human and political geography. I say 'a new world'; but, unless we admit that forgetfulness of the past comes to the same thing as wiping it out, it would be more correct to speak of the re-entrance of a very old world.

For the North Atlantic and the Norwegian Sea as far as the Arctic Ocean were very much alive long ago, in the days when Scandinavian mariners discovered islands there and made them the first colonies of the Western world. If the Vikings had been no more than pirates in a child's picture-book, the name 'Norsemen' would not survive in that of one of the French provinces. It was from this very province that the second wave – the first was the Crusaders – of French navigators and colonisers set out in the Middle Ages, among them Béthencourt, the legendary king of the Canary Islands, and Ango, who declared war on a king on his own account and made him mend his ways.

To Westerners and Nordics the Atlantic Ocean meant what the Mediterranean did to the Phœnicians, the Hellenes, and the Italians, and what the Indian Ocean did to the Arabs. Our North Atlantic, from the Isle of Man to Iceland, from Vinland and Greenland to Norway, Denmark, and Russia, was the metropolitan sea, so to speak, of a Scandinavian thalassocracy whose colonies reached as far as Moscow in one direction and the Two Sicilies in another.

The Hebrides remained Norwegian until 1266, and the Orkneys and Shetlands until 1468. The Faroes and Iceland became colonies peopled by Scandinavians about the tenth century, and developed so strong an individuality that a Norse nationalist movement made its appearance in the twentieth century, while at the same time Iceland obtained a regular Dominion status. In the Middle Ages, Greenland also was a colony peopled by Scandinavians. It was abandoned in the fifteenth century, and then, in the nineteenth century, was turned by Denmark into a prosperous colony with

a native population.   By the end of the twelfth century
Norwegians or Icelanders had discovered Spitzbergen,
known as Svalbard in the old sagas.   But the political
life of the northern islands during the Middle Ages
afterwards became localised, and they proceeded to go
their own way, outside the scope of modern international life.

When the great sea-voyages began in the sixteenth
century, the Polar seas attracted nations which were
too southerly to do more than establish seasonal settlements on shore in northern waters.   At this period, the
Arctic lands were looked upon rather in terms of the
ocean which surrounded them than in terms of their
own value.   It was a time of heroic voyages, which fill
us with admiration, mingled with a kind of horror,
when we recall the inclemency of the Polar seas and the
small size of the ships that adventured in them.

The second period in the life of the Polar regions
which now opened was dominated, west and east alike,
by the same search for a route to Golconda.   In 1500
the Portuguese Cortereal sought for the 'North-West
Passage' off the coast of Labrador, beyond the waters
where Cabot had sailed three years earlier.   The historical map of these regions next became covered with
English names: in Baffin Land, Frobisher, in 1576;
in Cumberland Land, Davis, from 1585 to 1588; off
the west coast of Greenland, north of 80°, Hudson, in
1607; at the entrance to the 'North-West Passage,'
Baffin, in 1615.

Between Norway and Greenland, from the 2nd
degree of east longitude to the 20th degree of west
longitude, the Norwegian Sea presents a wide channel
of communication between the Atlantic Ocean and

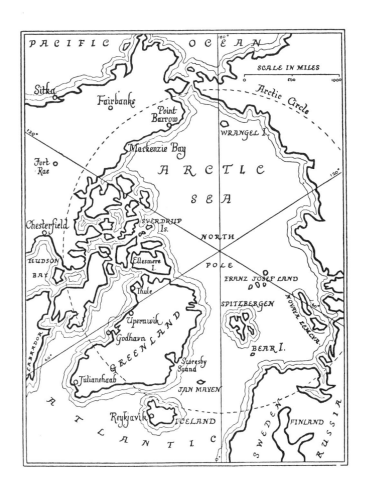

PACIFIC OCEAN

Sitka

Fairbanks

Point
Barrow

WRANGEL I.

Arctic Circle

SCALE IN MILES

Mackenzie Bay

ARCTIC

SEA

Fort
Rae

Chesterfield

SVERDRUP
Is.

NORTH

POLE

FRANZ JOSEF LAND

HUDSON
BAY

Ellesmere
I.

Thule

SPITZBERGEN

NOVAYA ZEMLYA

Upernivik

Godhavn

GREENLAND

Storesby
Sound

BEAR I.

LABRADOR

Julianehaab

JAN MAYEN

ATLANTIC

Reykjavik

ICELAND

SWEDEN

FINLAND

RUSSIA

the Arctic Ocean, by way of the Norwegian Sea, the Greenland Sea, and Barents Sea. This is the only sea-route towards the Pole which is not a mere corridor full of ice. It was here that, from the middle of the sixteenth century to the early years of the seventeenth century, English and Dutch steered northwards, over 'misty seas opalescent as milk.' In 1553, Chancellor cruised in the White Sea. In 1596, the Dutchman Barents rediscovered Spitzbergen and reached Novaya Zemlya. In 1607 Hudson, and in 1611 Jan Mayen sighted the islands which came to bear the latter's name. Far away, to the north-east of Siberia, the Russian Dejnev, in 1648, made a voyage, which was at once forgotten, from the Kolyma to the Gulf of Anadyr by way of the strait that was rediscovered in 1728 by the Dane Behring.

These voyages paved the way remotely for modern scientific exploration and immediately for the great fishing pursuits of whaling and sealing: the economic, one might almost say the industrial, side of these enter-prises of three hundred years ago. We obtain some idea of their hardships when we read the narrative of Dutch visits to Jan Mayen and Spitzbergen.

Jan Mayen lies on the threshold of the eternal ice in the neighbourhood of the junction of the 71st parallel and the 10th meridian, 'a boundary-mark of the world,' so wrapped in mist that, as Elisée Reclus puts it, 'you hear the land rather than you see it.' The island, thus difficult of access in the midst of the in-hospitable Arctic waters, is long and narrow, a sombre mass of recent volcanic rock. At its north-east ex-tremity, near the crater of the Esk, it is dominated by the Beerenberg, whose height a Frenchman, M. Paul

Duranton, attempted to establish in 1929, when he reckoned it as a little over six thousand nine hundred feet. Here were recently discovered the remains of seven Dutchmen who wintered on the island from 1655 to 1656, and died of scurvy one by one. The last survivor – he had the courage to continue the expedition's diary until he succumbed – died five weeks before the arrival of the ship which came to fetch them in the spring. After that Jan Mayen remained uninhabited, though whalers and sealers used to rest there for a few days.

For the seventeenth and eighteenth centuries marked a halt in Polar exploration, despite the hard work of whalers, sealers, and trappers, which was purely industrial. Thus, following Barents' voyage, Dutch whalers visited Spitzbergen so regularly that they gave the name of New Amsterdam to the settlement where they cut up the whales, extracted their oil, and prepared them for commercial purposes. But English and French sailors went too, and sometimes there were regular battles, in which blood was shed, for the best sites. The King of Denmark and Norway claimed sovereignty over the archipelago, and this was recognised, in 1663, by France, and afterwards by several other countries. Then whaling declined, Spitzbergen became forgotten, and it remained *res nullius*. Between 1750 and 1825, it became a fur-hunting ground of Russians, who often wintered there several years in succession. About 1800 the Norwegian whalers went back, and they, too, sometimes wintered to trap fur-bearing animals.

Then came the nineteenth century and the era of scientific expeditions.

Modern Polar expeditions

About 1813, revived enthusiasm about finding the 'North-West Passage' started a competition in voyages of exploration, which were made successively by Ross, Parry, Franklin, and MacClure.   It was not until 1853 that MacClure discovered the route so ardently sought for the past two and a half centuries, and then it was only to find it impracticable.   It was not until fifty years later that Roald Amundsen's ship, the *Gjoa*, went through the passage: the first and last ship to accomplish this feat.   Similarly it was not until 1878 that the Finn Nordenskjöld discovered the no less impracticable 'North-East Passage.'   Next explorers tried to reach the Pole.   Ships, sleighs, balloons, aeroplanes, submarines were employed one after the other to this end.   The American Peary claimed to have reached the goal in 1909.   It is, in any case, unquestionable that the Norwegian Amundsen attained it in 1926.

Scientific, too, were the Antarctic voyages of exploration: that of Cook, who reached 71° 10′ in 1774, and that of Ross, who reached 78° 10′ in 1842.   These voyages were not only scientific, but also, so to speak, more abstract than the Arctic voyages.

The North Pole is almost entirely surrounded by land, which forms a wreath beyond the 70th degree, with wide outjuts beyond the 80th degree.   In the southern hemisphere, Africa barely reaches the 35th degree.   The Cape of Good Hope is further away from the South Pole than Tangier is from the North Pole.   Australia reaches the 40th degree south, corresponding to the north latitude of the Balearic Islands;

New Zealand the 48th degree, corresponding to that of Orleans; South America the 56th degree, corresponding to that of Edinburgh. At the 45th degree of north latitude, land prevails over sea by more than half. At the 45th degree of south latitude, there is scarcely any land. At the 60th degree of north latitude, Asia and America are at their widest. At the same south latitude, the southern hemisphere possesses nothing but sea.

Neither the northern nor the southern Polar expeditions of the nineteenth century were of a kind calculated to appeal much to the general public, except when some dramatic episode popularised a fine adventure. Franklin's disappearance, the disappearance of the ship *Jeannette*, the *Polaris* ice-floe, Andrée's balloon – all these aroused a certain amount of interest; but fundamentally, perhaps, it was no more than popular interest in any 'sensational' incident.

In the course of the twentieth century, however, public opinion developed. In France, Charcot's methodical, continuous exploration was followed with respect even by people who could barely understand the bearing of it. Amundsen in Norway, Scott in Great Britain, Rasmussen in Denmark, thanks to their personalities as much as their achievements, became national heroes, and every American was proud when Commander Byrd flew over the North Pole and the South Pole respectively in 1926 and 1929.

Now that the Poles have been discovered and flown over, interest in exploration has become of a more scientific kind. As early as 1882, a new method of team-work made its appearance with the first 'Polar year.' On the occasion of its fiftieth anniversary, in

1932, this method was taken up again on a larger scale with the means and instruments now available. These 'Polar years' are inspired by the certainty that the keys to the secrets of geo-physics, meteorology, and terrestrial magnetism are to be found at the Poles. Moreover, to the theoretical importance of knowledge of polar glaciers and sea currents must be added its practical importance for fisheries.

The Polar regions possess not only an intrinsic geographical interest; they also possess an extrinsic value, so to speak, which is considerable. On their snow-fields, under their ice, a whole division of terrestrial life is prepared as though in a crucible. Just like the sea currents, the air currents of our climate cannot become known unless they are studied at their point of origin, which is either polar or tropical. No meteorological synthesis, no weather forecasting, except for the briefest period, will be possible until a regular system of observatories for making continuous observation has been established in the Polar regions.

Here, too, are assembled the best conditions for the study of the stratosphere: that kind of ceiling under which the movements of our troposphere occur. Professor Piccard holds the view that the next stratospheric ascents should take place in the neighbourhood of Hudson's Bay, which is close to the magnetic Pole. The situation of this Pole, in fact, does not appear to have varied for the past century from 71 degrees of north latitude and 96 degrees of longitude west of Greenwich.

The ionisation of successive strata of the atmosphere also can be studied under particularly favourable conditions in the Polar regions, thanks to the prolonged periods without sunlight and to the aurora borealis, which is believed to be due to electrical particles coming from the sun and attracted to the Poles by terrestrial magnetism.

This terrestrial magnetism has long been a subject of investigation, for as early as 1530 Alonso de Santa Cruz endeavoured to make a chart of its variations. Four centuries have passed, and the cause of these variations is now sought in the conductive strata of the atmosphere. Here is an example of the improvement of methods since 1882. At that time, readings of magnetic instruments were taken from hour to hour. In 1932, by a photographic process due to the Dane La Cour, forty instruments – half of them provided by the Rockefeller Foundation – registered the variations continuously in the different stations. Similarly, from a dozen observation-posts, thanks to the process of the Norwegian Stoermer, stereoscopic photographs have been taken of the aurora borealis, with the object of establishing its exact position in the atmosphere.

If the economic difficulties of our time have prevented the organisation in the Antarctic of researches parallel with those in the Arctic regions, at least a number of nations have taken part in the latter: not only nations directly interested in the Polar regions by reason of their geographical situation, not only big countries who share in all scientific research, but even little Continental States.

This fine combined effort of countries so different shows what the nations might do if they came to an agreement about scientific research and devoted a larger part of their immense budgets to it. The achievements of the Polar year of 1932, while they may seem somewhat abstruse, recall Henri Poincaré's words: 'The state of the world, even of a very small part of the world, is something extremely complex, which depends upon a very large number of factors.' Quoting this saying, Vidal de la Blache remarks that 'geography, being inspired, like its allied sciences, by the idea of terrestrial unity, has for special mission to inquire how the physical and biological laws which govern the globe merge into one another and modify one another in their application to different parts of the earth's surface.'

The Polar undertakings of modern scientists are the sequel to the daring exploration of the past. Just as that exploration developed side by side with whaling and sealing, so modern scientific study helps to bring the Polar regions within the world's economic life, and therefore its political life.

THE MODERN POLAR WORLD

Recent works by Rasmussen, Stefansson, and Rudmose-Brown have relegated the errors of our ancestors about the Polar ice to the past, just as Saussure's works did in the case of the Alpine glaciers. That great man Knud Rasmussen, who combined Esquimaux blood with his Danish birth, studied Greenland and traced the history of its people, described the Esquimaux of Polar America, and found traces of an old 'civilisation of Thule' in regions hitherto supposed to be barred to mankind. In these regions, where animal life was believed to be restricted to a few lower organisms and vegetable life to moss and lichen, Stefansson found birds and mammals, and counted so many as seven hundred and sixty-two kinds of flowering plant. Like Rudmose-Brown, for the old-time legend of gloom he aims at substituting the reality of a 'friendly Arctic,' whose herds of caribou and reindeer could feed millions of men.

Besides, modern scientific hygiene now makes living possible in Spitzbergen, for example, not merely for a summer stay, such as the old-time whalers used to make, but all the year round. Twentieth-century industry is developing the collieries of Svalbard and the mines of Greenland. It is not impossible that it may soon be extracting coal from the Antarctic.

But fishing remains the chief source of Polar wealth. Romantics describe whaling as a daily heroism – and almost as a thing of the past. To-day, in fact, whaling is an industrial enterprise just like any other, and, like certain others, it is threatened above all by its own activity, which is in danger of causing its raw material to disappear.

Fishing for the great marine mammals is nevertheless not so important as fishing properly so-called. Shoals of fish change their position in the course of centuries. Cod is becoming less and less abundant off Newfoundland; but it is to be found in quantity off the coasts of Greenland. French cod-fishers still fish off Iceland; but they also explore the richer waters off Bear Island and Spitzbergen, and even off the Murmansk coast, bringing life back to old whaling settlements which have been asleep for centuries. To Breton, Norman, Picard, and Flemish fishermen crossing the Arctic Circle is a commonplace of their calling; and to those of the northern nations the Polar seas are a second fatherland.

But, while grazing, extractive industries, and fishing

are giving the Polar regions an economic value which is bound to increase, another interest also attaches to them, or at least to the North Polar regions. Air navigation is creating international routes which will pass over the Arctic ice; and some people already see great air-routes meeting at the Pole itself.

Let us take, to begin with, the crossing of the Atlantic. The single 'jump' from one continent to the other, above the steamer-lanes which span the ocean at its maximum width, cannot for some time to come be anything more than a sporting exploit of no great practical interest. From the very outset, indeed, in June 1919, Alcock and Brown cut this jump by nearly half by crossing *viâ* Newfoundland and Iceland. Aviators soon recognised the importance of the Azores as a point of call; and the American Post Office plans an itinerary Carolina (or Virginia)–Bermudas–Azores–Portugal, whose longest stage, Bermudas–Azores, is only two thousand miles. We have seen the Italians follow, for squadron-flight purposes, the old route of the Vikings, marked out by Nature as a ford by its stepping-stones: Scotland, Orkneys, Shetlands, Faroes, Iceland, Greenland, Labrador. But, in order to avoid the almost eternal mists of the Greenland–Labrador crossing, what is now contemplated is reaching the east coast of Greenland at Angmagsalik, and flying straight across the *inlandsis* (ice-cap), Davis Strait, Baffin Land, and Hudson's Bay to Fort Churchill, already the terminus of an embryo air-line coming from Winnipeg across the prairies.

During the last few years the formula has begun to come into vogue: 'From Europe to America in two days *viâ* Greenland.' This formula offers the best explanation of the expeditions to Greenland since 1930: the German expedition, which cost Dr. Wegener his life; and the British expedition, whose leader, H. G. Watkins, one of the explorers who knew the country best, was drowned in a commonplace *kayak* accident. This expedition appealed to the imagination of the general public through Mr. Augustin Courtauld's solitary wintering on the *inlandsis*.

The Arctic air-route thus in course of study will be a reality in the near future. Hence competing claims and offers to purchase lands in the Arctic islands, hitherto contemptuously regarded as *terra nullius*. But this process of evolution is partly a sequel to the colonisations – some of them ancient, some of them modern – which, without anybody noticing it, paved the way for the present-day problems of Polar political geography.

THE DOMINION OF THE VIKINGS

In the summer of 1930, Iceland, an independent, sovereign State, having no link with Denmark other than a common crown, invited the world to a celebration which no other State will witness in our lifetime: the millenary of a Parliament, the thousandth year of the existence of her *Althing*. It is estimated that the number of visitors equalled one-quarter of the country's population; and, as it would have been impossible to lodge them in Reykjavik, in order to maintain the tradition of hospitality, in a country where the doors of isolated farms are open day and night to the unknown traveller, a camp for tourists was set up in the plain of Thingvellir, just as a camp used to be set up for the people at the time of the proclamation of the laws.

It was here, in this volcanic plain with its sparse

grazing, crossed by the river Oexara and bounded by Thingvallavatn, the largest lake in Iceland, that during two weeks every summer, from 930 to 1798, the leading men of the country debated the laws to be adopted by the Loegretta Court. From 1004 onwards, litigants came here from all over Iceland to seek final judgments from the Supreme Court, which sat on three tiers of seats in a circle in the plain. The people bartered, celebrated marriages, listened to the tales of travellers back from long voyages, and sometimes came to blows. The solemn occasion was that of the promulgation of the laws. The lava flow has formed two great fissures called Almannagja, 'the cleft of mankind,' and Hrafnagja, 'the cleft of the crows.' Out of Almannagja rises the Loegberg, the 'rock of the law,' whose acoustic properties are such that every word spoken from it, even in a low voice, is heard throughout the valley. It was from here that the laws were promulgated, just as they still are on Tynwald Hill in the Isle of Man, that other Viking republic in the midst of the British Isles.

After a half-century of silence, in 1843, the *Althing* met again; but henceforth it sat in the Parliament building in Reykjavik. It was a long way, too, from the laws codified in the *Gragas*, the 'Grey Goose,' to the very up-to-date legislation of to-day. Nevertheless, Thingvellir has remained a holy place of the Icelandic fatherland. If its 'general assembly' was in fact a House of Lords, with hardly anything democratic about it, it is no less true that it was in this plain that the grandmother of Parliaments -- their mother is at Westminster -- sat at the cradle of the first of Western republics.

Iceland, like Ireland, was one of the centres of our Western civilisation, and she preserved her pagan Scandinavian culture until modern times. To the descendants of the sea-kings she was not the last land on the verge of the Atlantic void. She was a stepping-stone in the middle of the ford by which men could reach the other side. Ingolf and Hjoerleif landed in 871 in the island, which was then abandoned by the Irish anchorites, who – like their brethren of the Faroe Islands in 725 – refused to live with pagans. As early as 982 the Icelander Eric the Red was in Greenland; and in the year 1000 his son Lief discovered America, where Thorfinn Karselfni attempted to establish a colony between 1007 and 1011. During these centuries of the Middle Ages constant maritime exchanges – with merchants taking the place of pirates – maintained uninterrupted contact between the British Isles and Scandinavia, Iceland, Greenland, and probably America, by way of the Orkneys, Shetlands, and Faroes.

Twilight fell upon Ultima Thule in the thirteenth century, and it lasted six hundred years. In the middle of the nineteenth century began a process of political evolution which ended in 1904 in Home Rule. In 1915 Iceland obtained a national flag. Europe, then at war, scarcely noticed the act of wisdom which was accomplished in the Far North in February 1918. Henceforth no link was preserved between Denmark and Iceland except the sentimental link of the crown. To-day Iceland is a member of the League of Nations.

Reborn Iceland now numbers one hundred and eight thousand souls, a larger population than she has ever had before, despite the fact that during the past forty years

some twenty-five thousand Icelanders emigrated to
Canada and the United States. Her healthy, energetic
people – not one of whom is illiterate – keep alive the poetic
inheritance of the *skalds*, and at the same time bring
the most practical turn of mind to bear on economic
affairs. If we take into account the fact that the
greater part of the island is covered by glaciers, lava,
and stones, we realise that the habitable regions and
the coasts have a density of population greater than is
generally supposed, and there are several small towns.
One never travels far through the meadows without
coming to a farm where a warm welcome awaits one.
The grazing is often very good, and the sea is as rich
as it could possibly be. The tourist traffic is becoming
profitable. Some day, perhaps, Iceland will exploit
her hot springs and harness the four-million horse-
power of her waterfalls.

Now Ingolf's island, the dominion of the Vikings, is
soon, no doubt, to find itself upon one of the great air-
routes of the world. To a little country, alone on
the verge of Europe, what more wonderful adventure
could be offered by modern magic ?

NORWEGIAN COLONIES

Officially, there is no such thing as Norwegian
colonies. Svalbard, the old name of Spitzbergen and
now its administrative appellation ; Jan Mayen, and the
Antarctic islets form part of the kingdom of Norway
just as much as the Lofoten Islands. In fact, the
Norwegians are specialists in the development of the
wealth of the Polar regions.

The story goes that, in the course of the three international conferences, interrupted by the war in 1914

and resumed in 1920, at which the attribution of
Spitzbergen to a European Power was acrimoniously
discussed, a Norwegian diplomat advised his Government as follows: 'If the archipelago is given to some-
body else, let us content ourselves with prohibiting our
subjects from going there. Since nobody can develop
it without them, the territory will have to be given
back to us. We have the best right to it – or, rather,
every right to it.'

The Norwegians, in fact, saw in Spitzbergen what
was to be the first in date of their modern colonies.
The Oslo geologist, B. M. Keilhau, was the first scientist to visit the archipelago in 1827. Captain Etling
Carlsen made the first circumnavigation of it in 1863.
Norwegian fishermen little by little explored its coast-
line. Nevertheless, the best map for fifty years remained that of an Englishman, the younger Scoresby,
and scientific expeditions went mostly from Sweden
until 1906, when Norway began to take a preponderant share in the scientific exploration of Spitzbergen.
The Norwegian Institute for Research in Svalbard and
the Arctic Ocean, founded in 1929, centralises all
scientific work in these regions, except for meteorology,
which is directed by the Norwegian Meteorological
Institute, and oceanography, which is under the control of the Fishery Administration at Bergen.

The Spitzbergen archipelago is believed to contain
five million tons of coal, and Bear Island some million
tons. Accordingly, coal-mining is the principal industry of Svalbard. As early as 1900, sealers took home
with them small stores of coal which they had found
flush with the soil; but it was foreigners who organised
mining, notably the American Longyear, who in 1905

formed the Arctic Coal Company, and this was what made Spitzbergen the subject of heated diplomatic conferences.

Spitzbergen's coal was of great value to Norway during the Great War. Iron and other minerals were discovered, and finally oil: all things which nowadays do not long allow a country to remain *terra nullius*.

The Norwegians argued that, if the coal companies were mostly foreign, their staff was Norwegian. They invoked their long record of voyages, their exploration, their establishment in 1911 of a wireless-telegraph station and a postal service, their whole work of organisation, which lacked nothing but diplomatic recognition. The Treaty of Paris, signed on February 9, 1920, by the British Empire, the United States, Denmark, France, Italy, Japan, Norway, Holland, and Sweden, established Norwegian sovereignty over the Spitzbergen archipelago – West Spitzbergen, North-East Land, Barents' Island, Edge's Island, Wiche's Island, Hope Island, Prince Charles Land, etc. – and over Bear Island. The treaty came into effect on August 15, 1925, and in 1927 all arrangements with regard to concessions were terminated.

In the course of the world crisis, Spitzbergen's coal production, which had risen to four hundred and fifty thousand tons in 1924, sank to two hundred and forty-three thousand tons in 1932. Only one coal company – a Norwegian one – is still operating to-day. But it has established in Spitzbergen a permanent population of five hundred workmen and employees with their families – not to speak of Bear Island's seasonal population of cod-fishers and halibut-fishers. It has been found that children born and bred in Svalbard develop in a normal way both physically and intellectually, despite the climate and the Polar night. It has also been observed that the Gulf Stream is at a period of increasing intensity; so the climate of the archipelago is tending to grow milder.

At the same time as she annexed Spitzbergen, Norway became sovereign of Jan Mayen. She has turned the island into an essential link in the chain of meteorological observatories, extending from Labrador to Scandinavia by way of Greenland and Iceland, which enable more and more exact weather forecasts to be made. These will be indispensable to the trans-Atlantic aviation of the future. The director of the meteorological bureau is invested with full administrative power; but his subjects consist almost solely of his own staff, who mount guard day and night over wind and cloud in a land which is, in fact, more isolated than any lighthouse in the world.

Such is the Arctic domain of Norway. We shall see in a moment how she attempted to extend it to part of Greenland, while, on the other hand, she surrendered to Canada the Sverdrup archipelago, discovered by a Norwegian expedition.

But the Antarctic, too, has attracted Norway's bold mariners, as do all frozen wastes, all seas lashed by the furious waves of the Polar regions. The Antarctic had become a happy hunting-ground for Norwegian whalers, but the destruction of whales has slowed down fishing. Official statistics recorded fourteen thousand whales taken in Antarctic waters during the season of 1925–6 alone. In fact, probably twice as many were destroyed, and restrictive measures – very difficult to enforce – were taken by all the States concerned.

South Georgia, the only permanently settled Antarctic land, is a British colony; but its great centre for the treatment of whaling products, more important than Port Leith or Olav Bay, is Grytviken, a regular Norwegian village.

Meanwhile Norway has hoisted her flag over Bouvet Island and Peter I Island. Bouvet Island, on the 54th degree of south latitude, is sub-Antarctic rather than Antarctic; but its climate is polar and very severe. An ice-cap covers the island in winter, and settlement is possible only in the summer and on the coast. A house built during the summer of 1929–30 was not found standing the next summer: it had been swept away by the storms. The summit which dominates the island is almost always shrouded in mist and cloud. Captain Rieser Larsen managed to photograph it from an aeroplane, and found that the mountain is an extinct volcano, with its crater full of snow.

Peter I Island, discovered by the Russian Bellingshausen in 1820, is scarcely more hospitable. It was abandoned for more than a century, until a Norwegian whaler circumnavigated it in 1927, and another made a landing there in 1929, two months after Norway had taken possession of Bouvet Island. The Norwegian flag has also been hoisted in the Antarctic between Coats Land and Enderby Land.

Such is Norway's colonial domain, where mineral and oceanic wealth compensates for the desolation of uninhabited lands, which only twentieth-century industry and science had the power to restore to the sphere of political geography after a prolonged eclipse.

MODERN GREENLAND : A DANISH CREATION

To-day a prosperous colony and the subject of a judgment of The Hague Tribunal of great interest to every colonial Power, Greenland was indeed the most forgotten of all forgotten islands when aviation brought it on to one of the international high roads of the future. Up at the top of the planisphere, hypertrophied to the point of absurdity by Mercator's projection, with its unknown north coast unmarked, Greenland reminded one of a piece of tapestry hanging from the mysterious frieze of the *theatrum orbis terrarum*. The average Dane took little or no interest in it, and the Copenhagen Government regarded it simply as a subject of activity at once philanthropic and scientific.

Extending from the 60th degree to beyond the 83rd degree of north latitude, and from the 20th degree to the 56th degree of west longitude – the north-west protuberance, however, extends beyond the 72nd degree of west longitude – the island of Greenland has an area equal to one-quarter of Europe. Except for a coastal strip a few miles wide, which enlarges only here and there and elsewhere disappears altogether, the whole island is covered by an immense glacier : the ice-cap or *inlandsis*, which Commandant Charcot describes as follows : 'A sinister desert, this glacier reaches an altitude of nearly ten thousand feet ; it is perpetually renewed, and pours cascades of ice from the coastal area into the sea, where they sometimes merge with the pack-ice of the fjords or the Polar basin.'

Hitherto the history of Greenland has been that of the coast and the coastal hills, where Esquimaux live on a soil with a dwarf flora, but with a fauna of astonishing variety: musk-oxen, polar hares, white bears, wolves, and foxes, not to speak of the lagopeds and other Arctic birds, or the innumerable denizens of the sea, beginning with seals and walrus.

On the ice-cap nobody ever ventured until recently. In the nineteenth century, people still looked back on Lars Dalager's achievement in 1751, when he covered a few miles among the glaciers to the north of Frederikshaab. In 1888, for the first time, a crossing of the ice-cap from one side to the other, from east to west, was accomplished on the level of Godthaab by Nansen. He had to change his route in the midst of crevasses, struggle against storm, climb to nearly ten thousand feet, and march for forty-six days in order to cover a little more than three hundred miles through glaciers where, in the height of summer, the temperature varied from 40° to 58° below zero. So we can understand why the inland ice should have remained a forbidden country ever since Eric the Red and his Icelanders landed in Greenland nearly a thousand years ago.

But the ice-free coastal regions, especially in the south-west round Julianshaab and Godthaab, experienced an active life during the Middle Ages. In the fourteenth century, these regions still numbered three hundred farms, two monasteries and sixteen churches, one of them the cathedral at Gardar, the capital, where the paddocks could hold ten thousand animals. Then ships came more and more rarely: perhaps on account of changes in the ice-system. The last ship from Greenland reached Norway in 1410. The race of colonists, if we may judge from their skeletons in graves recently opened, had degenerated; and perhaps they were massacred by the Esquimaux. In 1585 an expedition found the Greenland villages deserted. After that, only whalers occasionally touched the shores of Greenland.

A period of rebirth began in 1721, when a pastor, Hans Egede, set off to look for the legendary colonists. He found only Esquimaux, and devoted himself to their conversion. In order to save them from contact with whites, which he thought would be fatal to them, he requested the Danish Government to close the country against Europeans, assume a trade monopoly, and ensure a patriarchal form of life for the natives, thus protected against adventurers. Half a century later this policy was officially adopted.

So well suited to the country and the race was this method that the Greenland population, to-day mainly made up of half-breeds of Esquimaux and Scandinavians, rose in the past half-century from ten thousand to sixteen thousand souls. The 'Danish Greenlanders' live in sixty-two villages grouped in twelve colonisation districts. Every village has a shop and a pastor or a schoolmaster; every district has a doctor. Danish doctors and Greenland midwives and nurses have taught hygiene, and mortality has diminished. Fishing, hunting, and even sheep-rearing in the south, are organised and productive. There are hardly any illiterates. Pastors, schoolmasters, and officials may be mainly recruited among Greenlanders. The Danish administration has the assistance of elective councils, representing the villages, the districts, and the colony as a whole.

This evolutionary process has been possible thanks to the Government monopoly, which closed the country against foreigners, and thus eliminated alcohol and other causes of degradation. Pastor Hans Egede's successors have accomplished that most delicate task: making a primitive race prosper and multiply after the coming of Europeans. The system is justified in this case not only by its success, but also by counter-proof from the ruins found on the west coast, which had become deserted. In collapsed huts, which bore witness to former Esquimaux occupation, fragments of gin bottles testified to free contact with Europeans. Examination of skeletons may reveal more about the causes of the disappearance of former tribes.

Danish occupation has carried civilisation up to the north-west coast, and nomads have settled at Thule. To the east coast, which had always been neglected because it was less accessible, attention was first directed in 1878, when a commission was set up to direct geological and geographical research in Greenland. This led to the founding of Angmagsalik, the base of several present-day expeditions. In 1924, Captain Mikkelsen succeeded in settling ninety Esquimaux brought from the west coast on Scoresby Sound, at a point where there are a natural harbour, a stream, and good hunting-ground once populated. So he created a new centre of occupation.

Esquimaux and Greenlanders now prosper in places where their ancestors perished. They have become indispensable auxiliaries in the scientific exploration of the country. In geographical martyrology we should honour the names of Joergen Broenlund, who gave his life to save the scientific work of the ill-fated 'Denmark Expedition,' and Rasmus, who piously buried Dr. Wegener and then was lost on the ice-cap

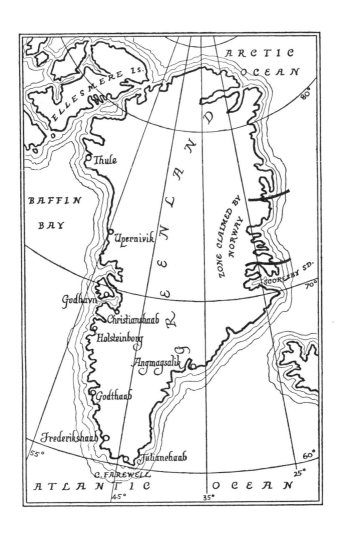

ARCTIC

OCEAN

ELLESMERE IS.

80°

Thule

BAFFIN

BAY

Upernivik

ZONE CLAIMED BY NORWAY

SCORESBY SD.

70°

Godhavn

Christianshaab

Holsteinborg

Angmagsalik

Godthaab

Frederikshaab

55°

Julianehaab

C. FAREWELL

60°

25°

ATLANTIC   OCEAN

45°

35°

GREENLAND

in attempting to bring back his leader's notes and observations.   Many others, who did not come to tragic ends, are unforgettable : for example, the inter- preter Hanserak and Olsen of Thule.   Besides, would learned, attractive, regretted Knud Rasmussen have been Rasmussen without his Greenlander descent ?

Thus Denmark is systematically developing the occupation of Greenland by the native race.   But her colonisation also has another aspect, which we may call scientific occupation : the only kind of occupation that is possible in most of the ice-bound island.

Cartographic and scientific expeditions have hoisted many flags on its coasts and on the ice-cap.   But, if one girdled the coasts with stripes in the national colours of the explorers who have studied them, the Danebrog would surround almost the whole island.   Since 1878 some seventy Danish expeditions have visited Green- land.

In 1910 Rasmussen founded, near Cape York, the trading-post of Thule, a regular capital for the Polar Esquimaux.   Its profits are devoted to the 'Thule expeditions,' which have revivified the study of the Esquimaux world.   In 1927 a Greenland Association was founded in Copenhagen, and expeditions became almost continuous.

The map of the extreme north, where Peary Land still figured as a separate island, was incorrect, and incomplete.   A young scientist, Dr. Lauge Koch, who had taken part in expeditions to Greenland ever since he was twenty, completed this map between 1920 and 1923.   Commandant Charcot said of Koch's achieve- ment that 'there is no "Polar," even among the most famous, who would not be proud of having accomplished it.' To grasp the twofold scope of Koch's work, we may refer to the passage in the chapter, 'Tempest and Famine,' in the explorer's narrative in which he describes his arrival at Cape Bridgeman. 'We had completed the circle, and, when the sledges arrived, I took out my little flag and planted it on the *vard* [cairn]. . . . I left the north coast behind me explored and plotted on the map. The goal was reached. The Danebrog had floated over the north of Greenland, and the topographical map, as well as the geological map, was provisionally finished.' Dr. Lauge Koch has since been engaged on a three years' expedition, with the assistance of twenty-four scientists, between Scoresby Sound and Denmark Sound. So the work continues.

THE DANISH-NORWEGIAN CONFLICT IN GREENLAND

Over this Greenland, which they had so patiently, so courageously turned into a prosperous colony and an outpost of science, the Danes assumed that the Danebrog would be left to fly in peace. But in 1921 Norway disputed their sovereignty over a sector of the west coast.

This was despite the fact that, exactly a hundred years earlier – and seven years after the separation between Denmark and Norway in 1814 – the Norwegian Storthing had declared that all questions relative to Greenland were settled ; and in the trade treaty of 1826 it recognised Denmark's commercial monopoly in Greenland. The Monroe Doctrine was in no way infringed ; for in 1916, at the time of their purchase of the Danish West Indies, the United States recognised

Denmark's sovereignty over *the whole* of the great Arctic island. In 1919, in a verbal declaration, the Norwegian Premier, Mr. Ilhen, did the same. So, in 1920–1, did the four Great Powers, Great Britain, France, Italy, and Japan, at the ambassadors' conference ; and so, too, did other countries.

But when, on May 10, 1921, the Danish Government issued a decree declaring the whole territory of the island to be under the authority of the Danish administration, Norway considered herself aggrieved by the Danish monopoly. In 1924, by an agreement valid for twenty years, she obtained from Denmark navigation, fishing, and hunting rights on the east coast. The next development was that a hunting expedition took possession, in the name of Norway, of the coastal district in which it was operating. The Oslo Government first disavowed this action ; but afterwards, as a sequel to a campaign carried on by some Norwegian newspapers, on July 10, 1931, it declared this region 'occupied' by Norway.

An extremely complex conflict concerning international law thus arose. The two countries were quite prepared to submit their dispute to The Hague Tribunal. Norway, however, demanded that, should the east coast be declared *terra nullius*, Denmark should recognise Norwegian sovereignty over this coast in advance ; a procedure to which Denmark obviously could not agree.

Finally, during the summer of 1932, the hearing began. The Norwegian Government put forward the following motion ; 'May it please the Court to reject the conclusions presented by the Danish Government ; to declare and rule that the Danish Government has no sovereignty over Eirik Raudes Land ; and to charge the Danish Government with the costs occasioned the Norwegian Government by the present hearing.' The Danish Government requested the Court to declare and rule 'that the declaration of occupation promulgated by the Norwegian Government under date July 10, 1931, together with all the measures taken in this connection by the same Government, constitute an infringement of the existing juridical status, and therefore are illegal and void'; and to 'charge the Norwegian Government with the costs occasioned the Danish Government by the present hearing.'

On April 5, 1933, by twelve votes to two, The Hague Tribunal upheld the Danish case, and gave judgment as follows : '(1) The Court decides that the declaration of occupation promulgated by the Norwegian Government under date July 10, 1931, together with all the measures taken in this connection by the same Government, constitute an infringement of the existing juridical status, and therefore are illegal and void. (2) The Court dismisses the contrary conclusions of the Norwegian Government. (3) The Court declares that it sees no occasion to depart from the general rule in Article 64 of the Statutes of the Court, according to which each party shall bear its own costs of procedure.'

This verdict was followed by an exchange of friendly telegrams between the kings of the two countries. The King of Denmark expressed the hope that the utmost cordiality should be restored in the relations between the two States. The King of Norway declared that his country would conform to the judgment of The Hague Tribunal. This, however, did not prevent certain

Norwegian papers from starting a fresh anti-Danish campaign.

From the juridical point of view, The Hague Tribunal's judgment is of interest to every colonial Power. For the Norwegian thesis implies the principle that, in any colony, any part not effectively occupied by the metropolitan Power is *terra nullius*, and that any other Power which obtains from this Power authorisation for its subjects to settle there, even seasonally, thereby acquires a right of sovereignty over the area in question. It is obvious what a source of conflict, even in the oldest and best occupied colonies, acceptance of this principle would mean. On the contrary, the judgment of The Hague Tribunal, apart from constituting a perfect juridical title for Denmark's sovereignty over the whole of Greenland, 'tends to lay it down that any territory whose major part is colonised by a State is as a whole under the sovereignty of the colonising State, provided that certain conditions are fulfilled.' (*Affaires Étrangères*, April 25, 1933, p. 242.)

From the point of view of human geography and political geography, the Danish-Norwegian dispute brings face to face two different conceptions of the colonisation of a country inhabited by a native race : on the one hand, onerous administration of a country for the purpose of exploring it scientifically, civilising its native race, and progressively turning that race into a nation inhabiting a gradually developed soil ; on the other hand, intensive exploitation of natural products, in the first place by hunting and fishing – a process of destructive economy, of *Raubwirtschaft*, as anthropogeographers call it.

At first sight, it would seem that these two types of

colonisation might coexist in Greenland, since the
region claimed by the Norwegians is uninhabited. But
here geographical analysis would have been essential
in order to enlighten The Hague Tribunal, if the
juridical texts, which alone were taken into account,
had unfortunately been doubtful. For here, side by
side with the external elements of the case, so to speak,
must also be considered the very delicate question of
the hinterland of a colony which lives above all by
hunting and fishing.

Hunters and fishermen from outside threaten to
deprive such a colony not only of its wealth, but even of
its most indispensable food-supply, by exterminating
terrestrial and maritime fauna.   In each of the whaling
seasons of 1929 and 1930, 30,000 whales were killed,
with the result that in 1931 whaling was abandoned.
As a sequel to their destruction, the massacre of seals
had already slowed down from 411,000 in 1925 to
169,000 in 1929. Now the east coast, thanks to the
difficulty of access to its coastal waters, constitutes a
seal reserve, where these animals, pursued everywhere
else, can find some security; and seals supply the
Greenlanders with food, clothing, tents, harness, and
tackle, not to speak of oil, with its many uses.

In Greenland, moreover, as everywhere else in the
Arctic, musk oxen constitute the great emergency
supply of food in hard times, which are always liable
to occur in these latitudes. Accordingly the hunting
of musk oxen is everywhere strictly regulated, and in
Greenland the Esquimaux never transgress the prohibition against killing these beasts, for they recognise
how wise this prohibition is. At Scoresby Sound,
and in the districts to which colonisation there will

eventually extend, the preservation of the musk oxen is particularly important. The trailing land in this region is really the economic hinterland of settlements there.

It is precisely this region which constitutes the Norwegians' hunting-ground. The herds, moreover, follow the coast, and to destroy them in one place means threatening the whole country with famine. In 1931 the Norwegian hunters at Mackenzie Bay killed one hundred and thirty musk oxen, most of them to feed their dogs. One of their firms offered a score of musk calves to European zoological gardens, where the calves could not survive. Their capture, according to Dr. Charcot, would mean the massacre of a hundred adult animals; for, when a herd are attacked, they form a square, with their young in the middle, and let themselves be killed to the last in order to defend them.

We can understand, therefore, why Mr. Ejnar Mikkelsen should write, in *Terre, Air, Mer*: 'It is quite inconceivable that the Esquimaux should be made to suffer as a result of excessive hunting carried on by foreigners. The civilised world cannot permit it. The Esquimaux are the country's own children; they possess the first rights over a region which offers hunting sufficient for their subsistence, and they should not be eliminated from their old fatherland.'

If the Norwegians had considered these consequences of their claims in Greenland; if they had realised that they were putting purely economic interests and human interests into opposition, they would certainly not have formulated these claims – especially as their economic interests in the matter were not considerable. Seal-hunting on the east coast of Greenland brought them in scarcely one and a half million kröner in

1925, and not even half a million in 1929. In the interior of the country a dozen hunters constructed eighty temporary huts in an area three hundred miles wide by sixty to one hundred and twenty miles long. Such was the whole extent of Norwegian 'occupation.'

In the agitation started by some Oslo newspapers for the purpose of claiming Norwegian sovereignty over the east coast of Greenland, something else was therefore involved. As in almost all present-day international conflicts, analysis reveals two factors – one psychological, the other economic. The psychological factor serves to arouse public opinion. Accordingly, it was represented to the Norwegian people that Greenland was historically a Norwegian colony, which became Danish only through the union of the two kingdoms under a common crown. Thus what was at stake was a regular national – or nationalist – claim, intended to wipe out the last remnant of Norway's hateful subjection to Denmark. The newspapers omitted to mention that the Norwegian colony in Greenland disappeared in the fifteenth century, and that present-day Greenland is a Danish creation.

The economic factor which counted most with the interested parties who manipulated public opinion was not a few barrels of seal-oil or a few pounds of musk beef. It was Greenland as a source of mineral wealth in the distant future; Greenland as a country of call for aeroplanes in the near future. Here we come at length to the real heart of the matter, and to the great causes which place on the political map regions hitherto utterly neglected by the Powers and by diplomacy.

The Polar regions in political geography

The Polar regions now raise international questions which more or less recall the 'partitions' of Africa and Oceania. Once before, in the Middle Ages, these regions ceased, at least so far as the Arctic was concerned, to be *res nullius*. Out of these old colonisations has survived an insular State: Iceland, to-day practically independent.

But then a period of indifference lasting for several centuries, during which Governments paid little or no attention to a clash or two between the rough fishermen and hunters of diverse nations, led to the Polar lands being generally regarded simply as coasts, in themselves of no value, where the temporary shelters built by cod-fishers, whalers, and sealers did not justify any taking of possession. Such shelters are to this very day the sole human achievements to be found on the Antarctic mainland and islands, and even in the Arctic; but twentieth-century Governments are no longer so apathetic as their predecessors about the North Polar regions.

The period of voyages of discovery in the nineteenth century left behind it the idea that any 'new' land should belong to the State of the 'discoverer' who had hoisted his country's flag there. According to this theory, Franz Josef Land, discovered in 1872 by von Payer, would have been Austrian, and the Sverdrup Islands, discovered by a Norwegian expedition, would have belonged to Norway.

But occupation has also to be taken into account. Wrangel Island, discovered in 1867 by the American Long, was occupied in 1914 by shipwrecked Canadians from Stefansson's expedition. Was it to belong to the

United States or to Canada ? It has, in fact, become
a Russian possession, just as the Sverdrup Islands have
been ceded to Canada. The doctrine which seems
destined to prevail over the former juridical and
historical doctrine is taking shape upon a natural
basis, a geographical basis. It is the doctrine of territorial dependency, resulting from geographical position.
Its application, for that matter, often coincides with
that of the old doctrine based upon historical title-deeds.

Canada is unquestionably the Power which first had
occasion to give peaceful application to this principle
of the possession of geographical dependencies. In
1922 she annexed Wrangel Island, off Siberia. Less
than ten years later she surrendered it to Russia. In
1900, in the course of an expedition in the 'Fram,'
Commandant Otto Sverdrup discovered to the west of
Ellesmere Land, some seven hundred miles from the
Pole, an archipelago with an estimated area of one
hundred thousand square miles, and hoisted the Norwegian flag over it. In 1930 Canada came to an
agreement with Norway by which it was ceded to her.

Thus two of the chief Polar nations, Canada and
Norway, have adhered by something better than words
to the theory of geographical dependencies. We may
regard the way as having been paved for this theory
some time ago, as far back as July 31, 1880, when
Great Britain transferred to the Dominion of Canada
her rights over all the islands off the Canadian coast,
with the exception of Newfoundland and its annexes.

At the time, these were simply rights over what we
may call a 'hintersee'; but they soon became rights
by occupation as well. Detachments of the Royal
Canadian Mounted Police are now stationed in posts

so far north that one of them, on Bache Peninsula, is within only eleven degrees of the Pole. Wherever Esquimaux live, these police supply them with food during hard winters; and they carry out regular patrols in the islands – the Sverdrup Islands among others.

So, in Canadian geographical circles, people smile when they tell the story of an American, Major Macmillan. He set off northwards to discover unknown lands, adorn them with 'sound and unquestionable American names,' and annex them to the United States. Even in the most remote islands, however, the major was welcomed by members of the 'Mounties.' Very courteously, they authorised him to visit their domain, subject only to the condition that he should provide himself with a 'permit,' which the Canadian Government would give him for fifty cents. It was not a ruinous sum; but it was large enough, so they said at Ottawa, to change the would-be explorer's ideas about the nomenclature and the allegiance of the Canadian Arctic islands.

The United States, in fact, have recognised Canada's rights over the islands to the north of the Dominion, just as they have recognised Denmark's rights over the islands to the north of Greenland; and they have declared that they regard Greenland itself, in its entirety, as Danish territory. In accordance with the same principle, the Russian Soviet Government has annexed not only Wrangel Island, but also Franz Josef Land, which it has rechristened with the name of Fridtjof Nansen Land.

These events serve to show that the definite doctrine in this matter will probably be as follows: that every State with a frontage on the Arctic Ocean possesses a natural right over all lands, islands, etc., situated within a triangle with this State's Arctic coast-line as its base, and the meridians touching the east and west ends of this coast-line as its sides. The apex common to all such triangles would therefore be the North Pole. In this way, States owning colonies in the Arctic will be Norway, Russia, the United States (Alaska), Canada, and Denmark (Greenland). The Americans would like to hoist the Stars and Stripes at the Pole, in honour of Peary; but it is questionable whether Peary ever reached the Pole.

The same principle can scarcely be applied to the Antarctic, surrounded as it is by immense expanses of sea. Nevertheless, two triangles have been marked out there, with the South Pole as their common apex. One of them has for its sides the 160th meridian west and the 150th meridian east of Greenwich, and for its base the 60th parallel: this is the Ross Dependency. The sides of the other are the 20th and 70th meridians west of Greenwich, and its base is the 50th parallel. Between the 50th and the 70th meridians, however, this base is carried forward to the 58th degree of south latitude; for otherwise it would include the extreme south of Argentina and Chile. This sector constitutes the Falkland Islands Dependencies, and embraces the great whaling centre of South Georgia.

Great Britain alone had thus reserved a colonial sector for herself in the Antarctic when Norway proceeded to take possession of Bouvet Island and Peter I Island. The United States of America may also be expected to claim a share in the South Polar seas and ice-bound lands. In the sub-Antarctic region, France possesses Kerguelen Island, Saint Paul Island, and Amsterdam Island.

X

ANALYSIS AND EXPERIMENT

So short a book as this cannot pretend even to sum-
marise all the phenomena of dissolution and evolution
which multiply around us in political geography, and
whose complexity, still more than their suddenness or
their violence, leads us in our pessimism – or perhaps in
the vanity which men always feel about their own
century – to imagine that the period we live in is unique
in history. I have attempted no general review of
present-day transformations in political and economic
complexes. I have, indeed, as far as possible avoided
dealing with certain major transformations whose
analysis, if it were to be complete and profitable, would
require a whole volume to itself: such, for example, as
the reorganisation of the Danubian and Balkan complexes, the continual process of adaptation in the
British Empire, and the activity on the periphery of the
Soviet Empire. I have preferred to take cases which
are relatively simple, but clear and characteristic, and,
among such cases, those which do not impinge unduly
on Western, and especially European, sensibility.

Accordingly, I have made a score of careful and
objective analyses – some of natural phenomena, others
of recent tentative experiments – with the object of
arriving at a system of classification, which has not so

far been attempted. Analysis and classification: such is the task of contemporary political geography. To breathe life into abstractions, to lay claim to the discovery of laws, would be a dangerous game here – the very game which has put *Geopolitik* outside the sphere of true science.

One classification is self-evident: on the one hand, the negative phenomena of dissolution or disintegration; on the other hand, the positive phenomena of evolution or reconstruction.

DISSOLUTION AND EVOLUTION

The first of these phenomena manifest themselves in four essential ways: first, by contests which reveal a kind of desuetude of historical rights; second, by a tacit abandonment of old treaties which have gradually become incapable of execution; third, by the rapid wear and tear of recent treaties; fourth, by the dissolution of Imperial States as a sequel to revolution or war, or sometimes even through a process of spontaneous disintegration.

Two cases typical of the challenging of historical rights are the conflict over the Chaco and the conflict over Greenland.

It stands to reason that these rights were neither more nor less contestable when Paraguay was quietly nibbling away at the Chaco, or before Norway came to realise the economic value of the east coast of Greenland. But analysis explains the genesis of these conflicts by revealing the economic basis which really underlies the pretexts invoked. In addition, it demonstrates the fragility of any purely juridical argument, which, in one of these cases, was shipwrecked on the rock of The

Hague Tribunal, and, in the other, led the armed aggressor to reject any offer of arbitration.

The feature which, in these two cases, presents a first-class interest – though it has hardly been emphasised – is that juridical or military attack on historical rights failed not only because the Danes and the Bolivians were able to produce title-deeds in good and proper form, but also because admission of the case for the plaintiffs would have meant the destruction of politico-geographical complexes which were the product of harmonious interaction between Nature and mankind.

The judges on The Hague Tribunal asserted the validity of historical rights; but they also asserted the right to life of a colony whose population could subsist only if the whole island concerned were placed under the sole authority of a State whose title-deeds were not merely juridical, but also economic, scientific, and humanitarian. Denmark's rights over Greenland in the twentieth century are based upon her rights during earlier centuries; but the two sets of rights are not identically the same. The present-day performances of a humanitarian government, such as Mikkelsen's colonisation at Scoresby Sound, no less than former title-deeds, 'sanction' its traditional rights.

Similarly in the case of the Chaco, it is not because it is impressed by the majesty of the royal decrees (*cedulas granadinas*) issued by the Spanish sovereigns from the sixteenth to the eighteenth centuries that general opinion has ranged itself on the side of Bolivia; for the cessions to which Bolivia agreed during her difficulties in the nineteenth century might have in-fluenced opinion just as much. What became obvious

was that, while it is true that the *audiencia* of Charcas
extended to the river Paraguay, it is also unquestionable that to Bolivia, deprived of access to the Pacific,
a frontage on the Atlantic is a vital necessity, and that
this frontage is represented by the Chaco, jutting
forward between the Pilcomayo and the Paraguay like
an inland promontory from which the Andean republic
can catch a glimpse of the liberating sea.

Here, again, old parchments constituted the basis of
law; but modern phenomena of human geography
constituted the guides in equity.   Nineteenth-century
Bolivia, with her Pacific ports, was a normal entity.
The humiliated and mutilated Bolivia of twenty-five
years ago was an invalid, awaiting cure or death.
Twentieth-century Bolivia is a healthy body in process
of rebirth, with the river as the essential organ of its
external life.   Moreover, while to Bolivia the Chaco is
'national,' to Paraguay it is merely a source of concessions to foreign companies.

The same thing has happened with antiquated
treaties as with old historical rights.   European nations
have had evidence of this fact in the case of the Capitulations, which for the past five centuries regulated their
relations with the Moslem countries.   There was
nothing in law to authorise the destruction of these
Capitulations.   They still possessed the same validity as
in the days of Francis I of France and Sultan Suleiman.
Yet they collapsed, as one mass.   Their dissolution
was, so to speak, a by-product of the revolutions which
have modernised the world of Islam.   In the same way,
Great Britain's old agreements with the potentates
of the Indian Ocean, the Persian Gulf, Iran, and
Arabia have gradually been annulled, as separate

sultanates and tribal territories merged into national States.

This dissolution of old treaties most often results from the dissolution of the empires which negotiated them. It would be in the juridical and diplomatic order of things that the successor States should assume the obligations of the old empires. But, though these successor States are composed in whole or in part of the same elements, they refuse to be bound in this way. The reason is that they are not simply fragments of former States, but new entities, with their own different organs and a new and distinct internal and external life. Geographical analysis shows this.

Such cases of the dissolution of an empire have been particularly numerous since the beginning of the twentieth century. One of the first – a spontaneous dissolution, so to speak – was that of the Chinese Empire. It was accompanied by European projects for the partition of China, which, after bringing the heirs-presumptive more disappointment than profit, failed completely, just as had been the case in the nineteenth century with the ever-open succession to the 'sick man' of Constantinople. In both cases, these projects betrayed illusions of the same kind, which methodical study of the empires concerned would have avoided.

Given such study, it would readily have been observed that the Chinese Empire consisted of two parts: China properly so-called, the land of the *Han* or 'Hundred Families,' extending from the Great Wall to Tonkin, and from the sea to the Gobi desert and the mountains of Szechuen and Yunnan. Outside this area, Korea, Manchuria, Mongolia, Sungaria, Turkestan, and Tibet never were Chinese regions, but frontier 'marches' where Peking's power dwindled steadily until it ceased to be more than nominal at the periphery. Thus the true domain of the *Han*; the domain which, if not that of their invertebrate political organism, was at least the one in which they swarmed and cohered; the purely Chinese domain was that of the western region, the great rivers and the sea. A map might therefore have been drawn up showing respectively the national State, against which any effort would be vain, and the imperial State, which was in full process of disintegration and left room for fresh domination. Similarly the coastal emporiums of Shanghai and Hongkong might have been recognised as possessing simply the character of trading-posts, whose existence made no difference to China properly so-called.

Instead, projects were made for carving out territories, from the coast inland, in the very heart of China, and they were regarded as paving the way for a complete partition of China. It goes without saying that these projects were based upon no study of the country or the regions concerned; for the smallest geographical observation would have demonstrated the absurdity of any such attempt. But all that the various great States asked themselves was where they were likely to find markets or be able to work mines and construct railways.

Quietly, unostentatiously, the Chinese organism – even though its slow reactions recall rather those of the lymphatic than those of the blood system – encysted or eliminated the foreign bodies which had made their way into a few points of its epidermis. On the contrary, foreign penetration through the periphery into the imperial annexes was continuous and progressive. The real dissolution of the Empire – not of the national State – occurred in the more or less abandoned outer domain; while the true Chinese State – which, adapting as far as possible a European expression to Asiatic individual and collective psychology, we may describe as 'national' – remained intact, amorphous and disturbed though it might seem. Politico-geographical analysis would have led to all this being foreseen. But people confined themselves to the study – and even this was sporadic – of economic geography, and to the negotiation of purely formal treaties, in which words excelled in concealing facts, and in which the Chinese could always get the better of excitable Europeans, whose game it was so easy to guess.

The European empires, for their part, have been reduced by the treaties which followed the recent wars to their national domain. It is for this reason that they have evolved into national States. Here, again, methodical study of the countries concerned would have spared many a disappointment. It would have demonstrated, for example, that you cannot put into the same category States so different as the Hohenzollern Empire and Herr Hitler's Reich. The lopping-off of non-German regions in 1919 transformed the nature of the German State, and strengthened its cohesion and homogeneity to an extent which more than offsets its territorial losses.

The reduction of Austria to a very scanty national territory – even scantier, perhaps, than that of Hungary, though she, too, was an imperial State – has placed her in quite another category of States. This is due, especially, to the fact that Vienna was the economic capital of Danubian Central Europe, and that the political dissolution of the Dual Monarchy was not in itself so serious a matter as the collapse of the *Zollverein* which that monarchy constituted before the war. In this case, the destruction of an economic complex has caused more trouble than the destruction of the imperial State. We can only assume that this destruction was undertaken by people guiltless of any such study as would have enabled them to foresee the disasters for which their diplomatic doings paved the way.

These cases of the dissolution of empires are naturally bound up with the recent treaties, which either provoked such dissolution or accepted the fact of it. It is for this reason that Europe is so rich in examples of treaties against which the losers – and sometimes the other side – are in more or less open revolt. Germany, of her own initiative, has torn up plenty of pages, and indeed whole chapters, of the Treaty of Versailles. So 'revision' of the treaties of 1919–20 has become one of the greatest sources of anxiety in the world of to-day.

This anxiety is not to be allayed simply by declarations about the sanctity of contracts and respect for one's own signature. Everybody is perfectly well aware that there are no international bailiffs to present writs, or international police to see that they are executed. Accordingly the French Senate, one of the most rational assemblies in the world, applauded M. Paul Boncour, then Minister for Foreign Affairs, when in the course of the Budget debate in 1933, he declared: 'While it would be madness, in the present state of Europe, to proceed to frontier revision, which might unleash the possibility of war, it would be no less absurd to proclaim the eternal and absolute intangibility of existing treaties.'

It is not by means of speeches at international conferences that we shall discover how far these treaties are inapplicable, and what changes in them are desirable or possible. South America has given the world two good examples of the opposite method, which it is equally dangerous to pursue: the Peruvian attack on Leticia, which was 'justified' by the fact that Peru's treaty with Colombia bore the signature of a fallen Peruvian Government; and the Paraguayan aggression in the Chaco, undertaken by a country which consistently refused to ratify the treaties negotiated with it, but simply took as much as it could get of the territory it wanted.

On the contrary, understandings based upon revision of texts or upon arbitration, as the sequel to local investigation and more general inquiry under the auspices of the League of Nations, demonstrate how useful it is to appeal to experts, such as economists and geographers, as well as to diplomats and jurists, with a view to the application of constructive methods.

RECONSTRUCTION AND SYNTHESIS

These analyses enable us to recognise five kinds of positive phenomena – in other words, phenomena of evolution and construction: first, the restoration of historical rights, *i.e.* the restitution, the 'disannexation,' of territory formerly seized by force; second, the reconstitution of national States; third, the creation of international territories; fourth, the organisation of territories by mandatory Powers; fifth, the constitution of synthetic national States.

Here we enter the domain of experimental political geography. We may, perhaps, feel that experiments of the same kind have often been made before, and that many treaties have contemplated something like them. But this is only apparently true. Up to the most recent international negotiations, there was nothing more than bartering with territories and their populations. It may sometimes have conveyed to the superficial observer an illusion of experimentation or synthesis; but any such illusion was due merely to chance.

In olden days, territorial and human factors were treated simply as pawns in a game of chess. They were moved about just as the players liked, and it never struck the players for one moment that the pawns concerned might have interests and feelings of their own, quite different from those of the 'high contracting parties' concerned in the game. In the twentieth century it has dawned on people that this may be the case. But they do not seem to have realised that, as a result, two factors have appeared that were previously ignored: the nature of these new elements in the situation, and their interdependence. Account has been taken of nationalities, and their history has been consulted; but the fact has been overlooked that this history, like economics, is conditioned by geographical environment. It has been believed that the study of *nationality* – an historical and psychological phenomenon – suffices to give knowledge of the *nation* and to prepare the *State*: but nation and State are complexes which include not only the nationality, but also the territory concerned and its innumerable kinds of interdependency with neighbouring territories.

Let us take the case of the 'disannexation' of Slesvig and its restitution to Denmark. This was a pathetic example of the ills which the best of intentions run the risk of engendering if they are not properly enlightened. The offer was made to Denmark of a province which had been hers; but part of this province had been germanised, and could now be nothing but a source of internal disturbance and external danger for Denmark. The error arose from the fact that, while historical study had been undertaken, study of human geography had been neglected. One might have hoped, however, that mere common sense would dictate that no such arrangement would be proposed without exact information about the present state of the territory and its population.

A restitution of territory may be of a more general character. Instead of merely restoring a lost province to an existing State, it may reconstitute an entire State which has been destroyed and bring a national State to life again. In such circumstances, however, very different cases present themselves.

Merely from the analyses which I have made in the preceding pages, we can recognise three types of such rebirth. First, we have the reconstitution of a State whose territory was entirely absorbed in a single empire: this was the case with Czechoslovakia. Or the territory may have been dismembered among two or three empires: this was the case with Poland ; this second case is the more serious, on account of the differentiation which may have developed among diverse parts of one and the same people. Thirdly, there is the case of the evacuation of an occupied territory: for example, Egypt. We have also witnessed the reconstitution of a former State, or the regrouping of a nationality, around a national territorial nucleus, as in the case of the Balkan countries, Greece, Rumania, and Jugoslavia. We may say that, so far as political geography is concerned, this is apparent.

But what is not apparent – and what may prove a much more serious matter – is the evolution towards national States resulting from the dissolution of an empire and its reduction to a national nucleus, or more than one such nucleus. This is the case with China, Turkey, the Dual Monarchy, and Germany herself. It was not recognised, and consequently many difficulties followed. For out of a collapsed empire may arise a potential force: a force which hitherto exhausted itself in the sterile oppression of border territories and non-national elements of the population. Hence we have had errors in Europe of the same type as those which preceded the attempts to partition China: errors which might have been avoided by the study of maps showing the political character of the different parts of the States concerned, as geological maps show the different kinds of soil which constitute their land.

Next we come to the Saar Territory: the only example in the world of a region directly administered by the League of Nations. By way of illustrating the evolution of diplomatic ideas during the past century, we may compare this creation with that of the neutral territory of Moresnet in 1815, the object of which was to place the Vieille Montagne mines outside the domains of Prussia and Belgium. The organisation of the Saar Territory was regarded only as a temporary economic necessity. To be sure, it was a question of assuring the neutrality of mines; but the reasons were quite different.

The Saar collieries were handed over to France in order to secure her the coal-supply that she could not derive for the time being from her own northern mines, which had been put out of action by the invaders.   Then it became apparent that this territory formed part of a natural economic complex based upon the wealth of the subsoil, and that perhaps the whole question had not been given the attention which it deserved.   A close interdependence linked the coal of the Saar and the iron-ore of Lorraine.   In Germany, on the other hand, rivalry had always existed between the Saar coal and the Ruhr coal.   The Prussianised Saar accordingly found itself within the French system on the economic map, and within the German system on the demographic map.

Such were the origins of the problem which the League of Nations, in the process of seeking a solution of a different problem, found that it had provisionally solved.   But the plebiscite held on January 13, 1935, in which the economic question was not raised, put an end, for purely sentimental reasons, to this experiment. The Saar-Moselle anthropo-geographical complex was broken up, and the Saar part of it was placed within the Hitlerian Reich.

The other experiments undertaken by the League of Nations have concerned extra-European territory. They take the form of mandates, and the example which I have chosen in these pages is that of the British mandate over Mesopotamia.   In this case, an analysis can be made with the maximum of objectivity, since we are dealing with an Ottoman possession which does no longer interest Turkey; whereas prejudice is almost always aroused where the former German colonies are concerned. Moreover, the Iraqi territory is the sole territory under mandate which has evolved into the creation of an independent State. Finally, Iraq takes its place in the contemporary evolution of British power as a whole between Egypt and India.

Nowhere has one a better right to speak of experimental political geography than in the case of this creation of a synthetic national State by the deliberate will of an experimenter, who groups its elements – territory, nationality, economic organisms – into a political complex. But the most interesting point is that the element of nationality, which, in the case of the reconstituted States of Europe, is usually predominant – at least in the intention of the theorists – presents in the case of Iraq only a secondary importance. Iraqi nationality, still in part only potential, is itself a product of synthesis. The elements which Nature would have taken centuries to bring together with a view to their useful reaction have been assembled in the crucible by an external human will.

In the same category of political geography it is permissible to classify Manchukuo, which also is a synthetic State. In the case of Manchukuo, Japan has given new life to an old land and an old people, and so, with the help of varied immigrant human elements, constituted one of her mainland 'marches.' She has established the administrative and political mould in which this heterogeneous dough may solidify into a resistant mass, just like sandstone, in which diverse kinds of rock may be recognised, but which nevertheless constitutes a new rock, coherent and distinct. This is, fundamentally, the natural process in the formation of nations; but in Manchukuo, as in Iraq, the will of an external power has undertaken to accomplish, within a few years, what is normally the work of centuries.

One question which arises, and which future generations alone will be able to answer, is that of the solidity and the durability of such synthetic States. Our period, for its part, must content itself with witnessing experiments which are more delicate and exciting than the more or less disguised annexations of the old-time empires, ranging from the simple subjection of territory by the Caliphs to the operations of Prussianisation or Russianisation performed by kings, kaisers, and tsars.

ECONOMIC INTERDEPENDENCE

The economic element is the most natural element, and the oldest and most durable of elements, in the relations between human groups, just as it is in the relations between individuals. It is an element which is to be found at the basis of contemporary experimental constructive processes, just as it was to be found at the basis of the old-time imperialisms. It plays a constant rôle in the static or dynamic formations of political geography, and every analysis in political geography recognises its presence.

The notion of economic interdependence arose in the consciousness of diplomacy at the moment of, and as a sequel to, the great treaties which transformed the world in the twentieth century. It is true that it has almost everywhere been very rapidly obliterated, and that by 1934 most States had reverted to the barbarous theory of economic nationalism. The first stage along this retrograde road was protectionism, which made it the ideal of every State always to sell, but never to buy. Since this ideal was unattainable, it gave place to the idea of the self-sufficing State. Certain European States have thus got to the point of subsidising the cultivation of beetroot, while the West Indian islands are removing rollers from their sugar-cane mills in order to reduce the percentage of extraction – and meanwhile the price of sugar remains as high as ever. And how many countries are now artificially maintaining a high price for wheat, while other countries are either burning the surplus of their harvests, or denaturing it in order to render it unfit for breadmaking ?

Some States, however, understand the working of processes of economic interdependence, and endeavour to turn them to the best account. But opposition to the normal interplay of the world's economic life is so fierce that to make these processes function properly requires political arrangements, which can readily be denounced as new forms of imperialism. Must the conquest of markets necessarily have as its condition the conquest of territory, and does merchandise require to be escorted by the machine guns of the State which manufactures it ? The result, in any case, is a dangerous entanglement between economics and politics. Accordingly, any political map should be drawn on a physical map, where economic factors have already been traced. For nowhere can the processes of economic interdependence be observed more easily than on such a map.

For example, study of the interdependence between tropical America and the North American continent explains what is called American imperialism; and study of the interdependence due to the canal between the isthmus and the United States explains the Washington Government's policy in Central America. Similarly, in the Far East, Japan's policy is partly conditioned by her need of opening up the continental markets and possessing sources of foodstuffs, minerals, and raw material for her textile industry.

A process of evolution less advanced, but of exactly the same kind, is the cause of the conflicts between South American republics. Again, one of the most perfect examples, because it is such a simple example, of economic interdependence between regions – an interdependence such as to require that the whole of a territory should be placed under a single Government – is the case of Greenland, where the very life of the Esquimaux population would have been endangered by the cession of part of the island to foreign hunting and fishing interests.

Conditions of interdependence of various kinds, but for the most part economic, and the necessity for reconciling their demands with diplomatic forms, have led to the creation of States which we may call intervening, either in time or in space; for some of them are only temporary and provisional, while others resemble the buffer-States of old-time diplomacy. Such were once the republics of Texas, California, and Hawaii; such to-day are the States of Panama and Manchukuo. We may put it that such States come to birth where and when annexation is impossible, while at the same time direct action by the interests concerned favours the development and prosperity of the regions thus promoted to the rank of States.

In addition, there are regions whose geographical position assigns them a special status. This status often arises simply from a division of labour in accordance with natural aptitudes. It takes imperialist ideas on the one hand, and nationalist ideas on the other, to put forward the claim that facts of political geography so perfectly in the order of nature are the result either of jealousy between States or the dreams of visionaries.

INTERNATIONAL EMPORIUMS

Such are the neutral emporiums, devoted to international commerce. They ought to be the happiest cities in the world. Yet sometimes, from Carthage to Venice, they have destroyed themselves by their political ambitions; but they have often been destroyed, as were the Hanseatic towns, for example, by the development of national States.

Europe, as it exists since the recent treaties, presents two examples of such commercial centres. One of them is maritime, and the other is terrestrial. The first is Danzig and the second is Vienna.

Statistics show that Danzig, prosperous though it is, would be much more prosperous if its status as a Free City, a modern Hanseatic town, had seemed so definite, so unassailable that Poland would never have felt the need for a commercial port of her own, if Danzig could have been Poland's Marseilles and Gdynia her Toulon. Statistics also show how Vienna, as the capital of a little national State, is suffering and becoming atrophied: an organ detached from the international body of which it used to be the head.

But German Nazi policy disturbs the life of Danzig

by introducing an element of agitation from outside, which would degrade this Hanseatic town, queen of the Baltic, and turn it into a secondary port of the Reich. Vienna, similarly, has to defend itself against external agitation from the same imperialist source, and also against its own internal partisan agitation. Here we have a twofold example of imperialist policy and national sentimentalism in opposition to the normal life of what we may call natural international emporiums.

Geographically, Danzig is the port of the Vistula Basin, and consequently of the Polish State, of which that basin is the centre. Demographically, Danzig is German. A Polish port and a German city, it should normally be external to both States alike: a Free City with commerce as its vocation, subject to no hindrance, economic or political.

In the same way, geographically, Vienna is the market-place of the Danubian region and of Central Europe. It is German in language, Austrian – one might almost say 'Viennese' – in nationality, cosmopolitan in its activity and its culture. It is *par excellence* a 'cross-road city' between the Germanic, Magyar, and Slav countries, and between the north and the south of Western Europe. Born to live independently of the various States of which it is the economic, intellectual, and artistic centre, no customs barrier should separate it from any of these countries, all of which would find it difficult to develop their own economic life properly without Vienna.

Such emporiums have existed in all periods and in all parts of the world. Their quasi-disappearance in our own time arose from the development of empires extensive enough to be able to claim that, in themselves, they constituted distinct economic organisms, and powerful enough to suppress the liberty of great merchants by annexing their free cities: convincing them that they were thus being restored to the political society of men of their own race. Now that national States have been restored to life, and the way is being paved for a society of free nations, their place must necessarily be given back to these commercial cities outside States. For national States have two essential corollaries: freedom of trade, and international emporiums – in short, Hanseatic towns.

The expression 'Hanseatic town' must not, of course, be taken too literally. The leonine methods of the Hanseatic league would not be either justified or tolerated to-day. But we can still transpose into our modern world the idea of communities essentially, if not exclusively, commercial. The relationship between a medieval Hanseatic town and a free port of to-day is much the same as that between Europe in the days when it was divided into principalities always at war, and twentieth-century Europe, in which a large number of national States surround themselves by tariff barriers and so dam the main streams of commerce.

It is one of the tragedies of our time that the revival of nationality, which can and should regenerate the world, should have been accompanied by failure to understand economic laws. This has led to the creation of local industrial activities which are artificial, and to the development of protectionism, which is responsible for a large part of the present crisis. Neutral commercial centres have therefore again become essential – if, indeed, they have ever ceased to be so.

In other cases, ports have been separated from their hinterland ; and it is indispensable that they should once more be linked with it. But if the port and the hinterland are not ethnically homogeneous, what solution can be found in a world which has made the right of nationalities one of its cardinal principles, and turned its national frontiers into economic Great Walls of China ? The problem is complex, for it is at once political and economic. The idea of commercial centres outside States and nationalities again presents itself as one of the ways which will enable the world to become organised for the achievement of the ideal of peace.

Frontier 'marches'

Similarly a type of frontier which was supposed to have been abolished has again manifested itself. This type of frontier is the 'march.'

Our time imagines a frontier as something like a garden-wall or a hedge and ditch surrounding a park : a real line, usually following a river or a chain of mountains. Every schoolboy knows that the earth itself changes colour from one country to another, as is testified by political maps, which give him an idea of the world almost as conventional as the maps of the Middle Ages, with the Garden of Eden in the middle and Paradise at the top. The best proof of this is the astonishment, and, indeed, the disillusionment, of any native of the centre of a country when he goes abroad for the first time, sees the frontier – or rather does not see it – and finds that the people on either side of the stream which bulks so large in history look very much alike to him.

But, while natural frontier lines are to be found scarcely anywhere – for rivers unite much more than they divide – on the contrary, as we pass from one human group to another, we find intermediary regions which really mark the end of one 'environment' and the beginning of another: zones in human geography having the characteristics of two countries, which they link and separate at one and the same time.

Such 'marches' become conspicuous when one studies the continental domain of Japan, or, again, the Western frontier of India. So far as Japan is concerned, it is evident that there is no frontier-line either beyond Korea, or beyond Manchukuo; but Korea was yesterday, Manchukuo is to-day, and Mongolia will be to-morrow, as a whole, frontier regions – in other words, 'marches'. In Manchuria, it is true, there was an organised frontier-line; but this was not the boundary between Manchuria and Korea, nor was it the boundary between Manchuria and China: it was the railway, the zone of the South Manchuria Railway, the backbone of the frontier 'march.'

To the west of India, the desert of Thar, then the river Indus, next the border mountains, and finally the Iranian plateaux mark a frontier zone about which it is impossible to say just where it begins or just where it ends. Again, where the Far East meets the Far West, the frontiers are not the sea-coasts, but the Pacific Ocean: that immense 'march' in which the Americans have their outposts as far forward as the Philippines, and the Asiatics as far forward as Hawaii.

Though topographers may be commissioned to mark frontier-lines on maps or on the ground itself, almost always the frontier really begins inside, and ends outside, the limits so carefully set. Such frontier-lines are necessary; but we must regard them as no more than what, in fact, they are: the present mathematical limit of the movement of States towards their periphery.

CONCLUSION

The essays which form this book are, first of all, objective observations and analyses: extracts drawn from general files for the study of political geography.

But, even within the limits of this book, they have already been able to lead us to a preliminary classification, more or less spontaneous, of certain factors in political geography: on the one hand, negative phenomena or phenomena of dissolution; on the other hand, positive phenomena or phenomena of evolution.

The first of these phenomena justify the title of this book to the extent that they convey an impression, at first sight discouraging enough, of a general weakening of respect for contracts. On the contrary, the second of these phenomena seem to herald new ideas tending towards security for the world. They enable us to catch a glimpse of a régime gradually replacing that of the old treaties, which were purely juridical, were supposed to be eternal, and could be transformed or abolished only by force – a new international order of living and evolving agreements; an experimental order, which may go as far as the creation of regular synthetic States.

Already the League of Nations has begun to turn political geography, to a certain extent, into an experimental science. Its experiments are usually possible only in the sphere of the most difficult problems, not to say the most desperate. It goes without saying, therefore, that we cannot expect these experiments to end in success always, or even as a general rule. But this fact scarcely detracts from their practical interest; for they demand methodical analysis of political geographical complexes, which hitherto has been sacrificed to analysis of juridical and diplomatic tests. In this way, we can succeed in isolating the simple elements which make up problems reputed to be insoluble. The first result of such investigation of the geographical, demographic, economic, historical, and political component parts of any problem is that, in place of dusty parchments in archives, we see cultivated fields, manufacturing regions, ports trading with the outer world – all swarming with human beings who say what they want, ventilate their grievances, plead for their right to live, and demand satisfaction of their hatreds: multiform life asserting itself, admitting no rule but that of texts born of life itself. The economic needs of nations, so often subordinated to the arrangements of politicians and diplomats, are restored to their proper place: the first place.

Thus the League of Nations raises to consciousness all that which, for so many centuries past, was repressed into national subconsciousness. This is, however, not always a voluntary act: it is not at all certain that the League of Nations ever intended to institute a new method, a scientific method, in international policy. Its views, at any rate at first, were mostly juridical and political. At the outset, it turned away from economic questions, because of an exaggerated, though very praiseworthy, pre-occupation of idealism. What has most often moved it to act has been concern for the salvation of oppressed peoples. But, as their salvation depends on equity, and therefore on the imposition of a natural order of things, the League of Nations has been led to study this order, and its work in this direction has become more and more definite. So it has come to be realised that the best way of serving those noble ideas, humanity and justice, is to make a bold, profound, and impartial study of hard facts.

Close as we still are to our first analyses, we can already observe that to every phenomenon of destruction corresponds a phenomenon of reconstruction. Whenever an historical right or a treaty falls into desuetude, beneath the momentary disorder we can see a new order germinating: a new order based upon new facts, or facts hitherto disregarded. To prepare this new order it is essential to make a close study of phenomena, a study that we might call political anatomy; and of such a study political geography is one of the essential bases. Sciences such as historical geography are now proving indispensable for the study of nations and States. For, without such sciences, the natural idea of international relations cannot become definite.

The twilight of treaties heralds but a short night. Then will break the dawn of new conceptions of international intercourse: the issue of fresh title-deeds, which the human race of to-morrow will respect all the more because they will be based, not on old parchments, registering victories by force or fraud, but upon real, concrete facts; upon the mutual actions and reactions of the earth and mankind; upon scientific analysis of these actions and reactions; and upon the natural sciences – economics, geography, and demography – upon history and upon political geography.

Here, idealism and disinterestedness are as essential as scientific objectivity. It is by giving ourselves up to the service of life that we can best accomplish, in all its magnificent plenitude, that task which destiny entrusts to every generation.

INDEX

261

WH   R/A15 DWLJ
                    Goblet